Thomas O´Beirne

A gleam of comfort to this distracted empire

Thomas O´Beirne

A gleam of comfort to this distracted empire

ISBN/EAN: 9783337272081

Printed in Europe, USA, Canada, Australia, Japan

Cover: Foto ©Suzi / pixelio.de

More available books at **www.hansebooks.com**

A

GLEAM

OF

COMFORT.

[PRICE TWO SHILLINGS.]

A

G L E A M

O F

C O M F O R T

TO THIS

DISTRACTED EMPIRE,

IN DESPITE OF

FACTION, VIOLENCE, and CUNNING;

DEMONSTRATING

THE FAIRNESS AND REASONABLENESS

O F

NATIONAL CONFIDENCE

IN THE

PRESENT MINISTRY.

Addreſſed to every ENGLISHMAN, who has at
Heart the REAL HAPPINESS of his
COUNTRY.

THE SECOND EDITION.

L O N D O N:
Printed for J. DEBRETT, oppoſite Burlington-Houſe,
Piccadilly.
M, DCC, LXXXV.

THE contemplation of our country's calamities is ever unpleasing. A people, however, can no more be rescued from their adversities, by shutting their eyes, than is a disease to be eradicated by scarfing up the seat of infection. To emancipate a nation, her misfortunes must be fought at their source; and fruitless is the hope of a perfect cure, unless the *cause* of evil be extinguished.

His mind must be singularly organized who can behold, without pain, the present condition of the British Empire. It is indeed no exaggeration to assert, that in almost every disaster that can afflict a state, this nation unhappily surpasses the rest of Europe. Public and private want; a monstrous mass of debt, and not the faintest hope of removing it; an immense fall in revenue, and a large failure of the most promising taxes; discontent and distrust throughout our dominions; coldness and disaffection in our fellow subjects; contempt and aversion in foreign nations; a precarious peace, and our

A   neigh-

neighbours arming at our threfhold ; ill humour corroding in all our dependencies, the
parent country rent to pieces by profligate
factions, and our gracious Sovereign infulted
upon the throne of his anceftors, by a daring
band of afpiring mifcreants. Thefe are a few
of the calamities of this empire, and fure
the review were melancholy, if we had no
profpect of redemption.

DREADFUL however as our condition is, it is
not defperate. We are unhappy, but not hope-
lefs. England feems to have been the peculiar
care of Heaven and miraculous interpofition
alone could have faved us from the perils
that from time to time impended our very
exiftence. But all paft dangers fhrink into
nothing, compared with our fituation under
the late Miniftry. It may favour of enthufiafm perhaps, but yet I cannot help believ-
ing, that the hand of Providence was concerned in forming the prefent Adminiftration, from whom alone this country has a
right to entertain any confidence of being
placed upon that footing of eafe and comfort
which a wife people fhould aim at.

AND does the reader think that the complicated miferies which have diftracted this
country during the prefent reign are attri-
butable, as fhallow men affert, to the incapacity and wickednefs of particular Minifters
or meafures ? Againft all fuch fpeculations
I beg leave, in the directeft terms, to proteft,
and

and however the fentiment I am about to deliver may militate againft ancient habits—
however it may combat with prejudices, fond
from familiarity and venerable from their
age—however diſſonant it may found to
thofe, whofe indolence or idolatry prohibits
the accefs of truth, whofe fixed errors pre-
clude from analyfing things in their na-
ked nature bared from the difguife of
fpecious eftablifhments—however it may be
fcouted by that impetuous faction, who
glory in curtailing the authorities of the
Crown, and degrading the executive government—whatever effect it produce upon any
man or body of men, I have no fcruple in
affirming, that *all* the mifery, diftrefs,
fhame, and difhonour of this nation, *fpring
from*, are *twifted with*, and *grow out of*, the
effence and *nature* of the *Britifh Conftitution.*

THE extreme delicacy of this fubject requires every poffible confideration. It is a
debt the reader fairly owes me and I demand it of his juftice. It is not reafon, but
prejudice—it is not the wifdom of men, but
their weaknefs I dread. Whoever goes beyond the beaten courfe of political enquiry,
has always much to encounter; much more
is the hazard in attempting the refutation of
long eftablifhed doctrines, and the expofition
of falfe and vicious fyftems, when thofe fyftems are fanctioned by the attachments of
mankind for a feries of ages. Here it is

that

that we are forced to confederate againft ourfelves, and that the pride of the human foul
is enlifted for its deftruction. The hardfhip
of afferting truths, which are not obvious, is
at all times great, but it is a gigantic labour,
when fpecious falfehoods, impofing knaveries,
and fraudulent ceremonies, which have been
reverenced for a length of time as folid and
fubftantial excellencies, are to be contended
with.

How many important tenets depend on no
other foundation, than habits of belief, and
currency of opinion! Few men can give a
better reafon for their religious and civil
creed than this fimply, that their fathers
profeffed the fame faith—and though it is
prepofterous that a religion or a government
muft be the beft in the world only becaufe
our anceftors thought them fo; how feldom
is it that either is vindicated upon wifer principles and indeed how rare to find any one
who can abide the difquifition with the temper or fobernefs of a rational being!

A DELUGE of grofs delufion covered all
Chriftendom for above a thoufand years.
What anathema's, thunders, deftructions
were levelled againft any perfon who ftrove
to emerge from this gulph of darknefs. All
the Divinities of Heaven were centered in
the perfon of that Pope, who has fince been
a compendium of all that is abominable upon
earth. Such *was* the effect of inveterate cuftom,

tom, fuch *is* the effect of liberal conviction ; the reform of religious error was rapid and decifive in this ifland, and civil error will, I truft, be abolifhed with the fame expedition and fpirit.

LIBERTY founds well. The very name of the Britifh Conftitution bewitches and fafcinates men. It is not admiration they feel, it is idolatry. It is not the cool worfhip of reafonable creatures, it is the furious bigotry of defperate enthufiafts.

BUT let us not be debauched by figures! Let us take off the veil that fhrouds this Pagod—behold the oracle difrobed of its mantle, and what a combination of deformity prefents itfelf! What a mafs of fraud, impofture, ignorance, inconfiftency, folly, corruption, and violence, make up this vaunted fyftem on which this nation prides itfelf, and for which we are fo juftly the butt of Europe!

THE boafted fuperiority of the Britifh Conftitution is faid to confift in its blending a portion of the three ordinary forms of government.—True, it contains certain qualities of each, and this very commixture it is, that conftitutes its vice and renders it the very worft form of civil polity in the univerfe.

AN ariftocracy is always haughty, imperious, and auftere. Infinite mifchief grows out of fuch a government, even if it were

A 3 pure

pure and unmixed. A democracy is ever turbulent, untractable, and violent ; by its very genius, it produces eternal ftrife and tumult, though it were refifted by no other power whatever.—But curfed with both thefe forms, and poffeffing no ufeful, no vigorous, or efficient particle of a monarchy, the Britifh Government is at once the moft miferable and ridiculous fyftem that can be imagined. Our hiftory is nothing but a feries of cabal, difcord, fedition, and rebellion to the Prince ; of tyranny, treachery, and cruelty towards each other. In other free governments the rage of parties and the violence of factions fometimes ceafe, and the publick enjoy a cafual hour of tranquillity. But with us, diffentions, animofities, and outrages are perennial. Looking back for a century, we fee from the daring fpirit that fprings from this conftitution, the beft monarchs counteracted in their laudable views of abridging the pernicious powers of the people and in ftrengthening and eftablifhing the Royal authority, whofe feeblenefs and inefficacy encouraged thefe ftruggles in the fubjects. One amiable Prince, (whom we have fince juftly canonized) perifhed upon a fcaffold and another with his family expelled the Crown for ever, contrary to every law and againft the ordinations of Heaven, (for who can doubt that Sovereigns are facred, and that government is a right divine.) The

land

land ftreaming with rivers of blood, and cruelty and carnage defolating thefe miferable
iflands upon pretences of *liberty*. In the prefent century, we have had lefs flaughter and
ferocious barbarity it is true, but not more
comfort. The block had luckily gone far
in the annihilation of moft of our great families and the Crown, it is true, has had
little trouble in latter times from the ariftocracy. A new race of nobles, fuitable to the
views of the Court, was erected by the new
family that was called to the throne (whofe
right is as holy and whofe perfons are juft
as facred as the former family.)--But by the
people, the governing authority has been
more thwarted, baffled, refifted, and reviled,
than ever. Oppofition grew fyftematic and
was openly proclaimed in the Sovereign's
teeth. A favourite Minifter has been forced
from the King's council with as little cere-
mony as they hang a highwayman, and
party violence and villainy carried to extre-
mities fcarcely credible.

WE are told, that each of the three eftates
has its feparate properties, and that the Conftitution fubfifts by the tenacious prefervation
of thefe properties. But we find in fact, that
thefe properties are fo undefined, fo bewil-
dered in ambiguity, that they become an
endlefs fource of wranglings and diffentions.
The exclufive right of the Commons yefterday, is the clear right of the Lords tomor-
A 4 row.

row. Difcuffions and controverfies fucceed, and the nation is kept in hot water, by a clafhing of jurifdiftions, and a war of declarations and manifeftos. The Crown which is the natural feat of all powers, privileges, and properties, is put behind the curtain in many of thefe difputes and the King's name perhaps never once mentioned, when in faft he is principal in the caufe and planned the whole litigation. The equipoife, or to ufe the new word, the balance, of the fyftem has never exifted at all; for nothing can be more directly repugnant than the theory and practice of this Conftitution.

It is in truth a machine conftrudted upon principles fo whimfical and extravagant—compofed of materials fo oppofite and difcordant—with means fo inadequate to the objects, and with objects fo unaccomplifhable by any poffible operation of the inftruments—fo confufed, fo complicated, fo contradictory, that no ftate pilot ever condudted it with harmony in the movements, or with fuccefs in the execution of its functions for any length of time.

The end of human nature is happinefs, and the perfection of human polity is the promotion of it. That government is moft complete, whofe fubjects are moft contented; murmurs and miferies are the natural and eternal produce of our fyftem, and by this infallible teft, it is by much the moft pernicious government of Europe.

WITH

WITH thorough confidence therefore it is, that I submit to thofe who have fagacity to penetrate this mafs of fatal foolery and liberality to own their conviction, whether it is not the true intereft of the Englifh nation, that this fyftem of vexation, inconfiftency, impofture, venality, corruption, and perfidy fhould be utterly demolifhed.—And that all the powers of all its various parts be concentrated in their rightful and genuine depofitory—*the perfon of the King.*

THE Minifters that beft promote this GREAT CAUSE, are moft entitled to our confidence and gratitude. Our abhorrence alone is due to thofe who thwart it.

IN THIS COUNTRY there is a fet of men who, upon this wife and virtuous principle deferve the fincere reverence of this nation. A fet of men, who (above the feelings that counteract the wifhes of ordinary people, at the hazard of their individual fafety, the certain lofs of private good fame and public reputation, under the weight of national execration and againft an ocean of obftacles) have fteadily and uniformly fought the happinefs of the people of England, in their own defpight. Even when covered with public infamy and perfecuted by popular hatred, they have in the meek fpirit of the divinity, cried out " *We forgive them, they know*

know not what they do," and in thofe very moments exerted their beft faculties to redeem us from the mileries which are our inheritance under this form of government and which muft be our lot until the radical overthrow of the Englifh Conftitution is happily accomplifhed.—The reader cannot well be ignorant that I mean the *King's friends*, or to fpeak more in technicals, *the fecret advifers of the Crown.*

HISTORY records fome inftances of a generous felf-devotion in bodies of men of the antient world.---In modern times certainly nothing has occurred worthy to be compared with the illuftrious advocates of *our* welfare. In the conduct of thofe mentioned in Roman ftory, there is without doubt much to be commended, but it fhould be remembered that the greateft of them, the Horatii, the Decii, the Fabii, were backed by the people and incited by the fure applaufe of their *Co-temporaries* ; whilft on the contrary the King's friends are detefted by the prefent generation, and are animated only with the dry confidence of *future* fame. A view of their *objects* elevates the latter into a fplended fuperiority. The Roman worthies ftruggled only for the *glory* and *liberty* of their country (which the Zealots for free fyftems think fynonimous) whilft the King's friends purfue the *folid happinefs* of the peo-

ple

ple in defiance of a hoft of doctrines and a mountain of prejudices, which great writers (Lock, Selden, Sydney, Somers, &c.) and the hereditary infanity of Englifhmen have rendered revcrend and holy. Oppofed by greater impediments, the title of the latter to immortality is therefore greater and more decided.

It were a tedious talk to detail all the labours of thefe good men for this great end. Much of their atchievements muft have reached the knowledge of every man in this country, but their previous feats are reduced to nothing when compared with their exploits during the laft year. To thofe I mean to confine myfelf.

THE full half of this mighty undertaking was effected at once in the fall of the late and the rife of the prefent Adminiftration.

It is a general opinion that Fox's India bill was thrown out, not from its defects but as a means of fubverting the Miniftry,—this opinion, popular as it is, I beg leave to deny. It is not the fall of any particular Minifter that can confummate the great work of our redemption from this conftitution. That fcheme had been often tried before and tried in vain. The CAUSE was but flightly promoted by fuch events, and conviction in the country progrefsed very flowly.

UNLESS the defeat of obnoxious Minifters

was

was accompanied by circumſtances that tended to expoſe the falſe principles, and un-ravel the impoſtures of the Conſtitution, the whole were a raſh and impotent experiment. Milder methods than the loſs of the India bill might have vanquiſhed the Portland Adminiſtration, but that, of all others, was the beſt, becauſe in that daſhing meaſure many leading and capital ends were com-pleated at a ſingle ſtroke.

THE ruin of their enemies was, I am per-ſuaded, a ſmaller motive with the King's friends, than convincing mankind by their *manner* of overthrowing the India bill, of the rank abſurdity of theſe two fundamental maxims of the Britiſh Conſtitution—viz. That each branch of the three eſtates *muſt* be independent of the reſt—And that the Crown *can* never intefere with the delibera-tions of Parliament. The lie direct was given both to the *muſt* and the *can*. For the Houſe of Lords *was not* independent, and the Crown *did palpably* interfere.

OBSERVE how much they accompliſhed in this act—They overturned an obnoxious Adminiſtration, formed one exactly ſuitable to their own views, and demonſtrated the impoſture of theſe two primary maxims.

FOR *centuries* it has been thought, that the King's diſcretion in appointing Miniſters was governed by the opinion of the Houſe of Commons; and *ſince the revolution*, it has

has been received like pofitive law. The repugnance of this rule to all the objects of the King's friends, on the face of it, fhews the neceffity of its total extinction. In this perfuafion, the foul of the doctrine was attacked in *argument*, and in *fact* it was utterly done away, for whilft the Commons were loading the Miniftry with cenfure upon cenfure, the King was loading them and their connections with honours and emoluments.

A REFORM of the Houfe of Commons has been for fome time popular in this country. If by any miracle that fcheme fhould take place and that the Houfe of Commons *continued* to preferve its weight in our fyftem, the reader muft fee the total inefficacy of all the efforts of the King's friends againft the Conftitution. Perfuaded of this, they attacked the popular branch with fo fignal a fpirit, fo compleatly difgraced its privileges, and eftablifhed its debility and contempt, in a manner fo decifive and exemplary, that if the moft fafcinating theory of the wifeft of thefe reformers were adopted to-morrow, not the leaft foundation is there of an apprehenfion from the authority of the Lower Houfe, or its refiftance to the laudable operations of the King's Friends. And the beauty of this atchievement was, that the degradation of the Commons was principally effected by the aid and concurrence

of

of the moſt furious of theſe reformers. The
project indeed exiſted for ſome time.

THAT great and good man, (whoſe ab-
ſence from our public counſels would be irreparable, if his genius did not inſpire the
Miniſtry) the Earl of Shelburne, has made
an early figure in this eſſential part of this
great undertaking. That unparalelled ſtateſ-
man told the Houſe of Lords,* that an old
man, who lived ever ſince Queen Anne's
time, *actually declared*, " that the Commons
had gained *too much* in the ſcale of the Conſtitution !" Who this old man was we never
heard, but his opinion proves him a wiſe
old man—A good old man he muſt be, for
he was Lord Shelburne's friend !

BY the practice and theory of this Conſtitution, (for this is one of the few inſtances
where they do not vary) the two Houſes
have certain authorities, independent of each
other and diſtinct from their legiſlative
functions. The Lords have a dernier and
final power of judication. The Commons
the power of granting the public money.

MONEY is the ſinew of civil operations;
abilities and ingenuity are fruitleſs without
it. What ſucceſs could the King's friends
expect whilſt this great right remained in-
tangible in the Houſe of Commons ? They

---

* UPON a motion of his own in May 1783, recommending,
" that in augmenting the public debt, care ſhould be taken to
" leſſen it."

began

·began accordingly with *dividing* it, as the fureft method of taking it away altogether in due time.

THE debate upon Lord John Cavendifh's loan difcovered the firft *ferious* proof of this great defign. The Peers Shelburne, Thurlow, Richmond, and feveral of the minor clafs of thefe illuftrious confederates, in the plaineft language denied this privilege of the Commons. They declared its affumption to be an *ufurpation*, and afferted *their equal* power of originating money bills whenever they pleafed. This was only a prelude to the grand fcenes that fucceeded.

BEFORE the Chriftmas recefs of 1783, the Houfe of Commons refolved an *opinion* concerning the exercife of a *difcretionary* power in the Board of Treafury touching a particular branch of *money*. The Houfe of Lords in fome time after declared that this refolution of the Commons was a breach of the law of the land and agreed in a ftring of motions, the fubftance of which was, a direct charge upon the Lower Houfe of *violating the Conftitution*, in giving their *opinion* concerning this *difcretion* in the Treafury upon the fubject of *money*. The Lords ufed no manœuvre, no intrigue, no underhand trick in this bufinefs, but openly, and in the face of day, publifhed this gallant corollory of that celebrated refolution of the Long Parliament,

Parliament, which declared the Houfe of Lords ufelefs.

Two great ends were gained to the *King's friends* in this bufinefs. The fundamental principles of the Houfe of Commons were cut up by the roots, and the fallacy of our fyftem was demonftrated in this proof of the doubtfulnefs and incertitude of Parliamentary Rights,—when in the year 1784 one branch folemnly proclaims that the other branch had broken the law of the land and violated the Conftitution, in doing *that which has been their conftant practice for a thoufand years*—NEVER QUESTIONED, NEVER DISPUTED BEFORE THAT MOMENT.

THERE is now no impediment to the execution of all the money tranfactions of this nation in the Upper Houfe; and perhaps, Lord Ferrers, who is a mafter in finance and a friend to the King's friends, may open *his* budget this winter in that auguft affembly, if indeed he can fpare time from the improvement of the navy.

THUS having confirmed, that the Commons of England had not half the influence of the Common Council of London, upon the fituation of a Minifter—and having deprived them of their vaunted power, of *granting money*, there remained only to degrade their moral character to the loweft extremity. In this the fuccefs of the King's friends was marvelous.

THE majority that condemned the miniftry was one hundred and thirty, before the
recefs. But by the abilities of *him* "wondrous
him, that miracle of men!" By the magic
aid of that immaculate man, who, although
now covered with infamy by blind unthinking
people, although the rafhnefs of this generation may ftamp him as the vileft and bafeft
of mankind, will live to be the idol of futurity,
and will go down to the after ages, fteeled
in immortality—I mean Jack Robinfon:

---By him the ruftinefs of the commons
was fo refined, their paffions fo purged, their
pride fo tamed, the conquefts of the *faction*
grew fo fruitlefs, and all their glories fo fa-
ded, that in the fhort fpace of two months
this majority that would fcale Heaven, was fo
pared down, that the tottering fabrick of this
deftructive Conftitution was upheld only by
the folitary vote of an *individual*, and he
was not an Atlas.---The generous John
Elewes*.

DURING this ftruggle no part of the ordinary bufinefs of the nation was tranfacted.
The Commons fat only to wafte their animal fpirits in voting cenfures upon the miniftry. The Lords fat only to vote the Commons a parcel of fcoundrels. Vanquifhed in

* MR. ELEWES fometimes voted with the Miniftry and fometimes againft them. His Judgment happened to vibrate with
the oppofition when the famous reprefentation of the commons
was carried by a majority of *one*.

their

their own victories, the *faction* at length
called upon the King's friends to bring forward the King's bufinefs, and pledged themfelves not to oppofe it. The majority being
thus reduced, the firft thing looked for was
a motion to refcind the refolutions that condemned the Adminiftration.---For even *then*
the exiftence of the Votes of cenfure and
of the miniftry was deemed incompatible,
fuch is the force of conftitutional idolatry!

HERE I feel my incapacity to do juftice
to the King's friends. This fatal contamina--
ting conftitution had much to plead in its
behalf. Its age—our fuccefs—our national
renown under it—habits of attachment that
grew into enthufiafm—Thefe made its demolition a ftupendous undertaking. The hazard of the attempt—the infamy, the ruin
of its mifcarriage, naturally induced fufpicions
of the ferioufnefs of Miniftry. But their
conduct in this great crifis difpelled all doubt,
and they ftood confeffed the chofen few, deftined by Providence to redeem this nation
from its prefent pernicious Government—the
mighty magicians that were to burft that en-
chantment, which kept our forefathers
chained in the bondages of civil liberty ! !

To refcind the refolutions—no—that were
to reftore things to their ancient level and to
re-eftablifh that damnable doctrine that the
the opinion of the Commons could in any degree affect the miniftry. That indeed were
a di-

a direct controverfion of this aufpicious project and plunging us back into all the horrors
of the conftitutional fyftem again. The Minifter's majority in the new houfe is near 200,
and to crown the degradation of the democra-
tic branch, the refolutions ftill ftand upon their
journals, in ftatu quo, a ftaring image of their
own difgrace and a fplendid monument to the
admiring world of the rapid progrefs of human reafon and the fignal victories it has acquired in fo fhort a time in thefe Iflands, over
that mountain of prejudice and bigotry which
grew out of the very texture of the Englifh
conftitution !!

As if *apprehenfive* that the Commons might
obliterate this living fymbol of their fhame,
the King's friends took the moft moft infallible method to prevent it. After the houfe
declared a determination to forward the public bufinefs the wifdom was evident of
dropping all bufinefs of every kind, and when
the contempt of the Commons was recorded and eftablifhed, the natural fate of fuch
an affembly befel them. They were fent
packing like a fet of reprobates round that
country, " from whofe bourne fo few of
" them returned,"—They were diffolved.

I AM prepared to meet all the objections of
the Whigs, to the diffolution (apologizing to
the reader at the fame time for defcending to
notice the fnarling of that vile *faction.)*

IN the firft place, they fay it was wicked to

B 2   diffolve

diffolve the Parliament, becaufe the King folemnly pledged himfelf not to diffolve it. The
very nature of this objection is the ftrongeft
juftification of the meafure. That his Majefty
pledged himfelf from his throne *againft* it, is
furely the beft of all reafons *for* it. Even a
King of France, adds the *faction, fo* committed to the moft paltry Parliament in any of
his Provinces, would fooner have died than
fully his honour by fuch a breach of faith.
Perhaps he might, and in that very view,
the diffolution has tenfold merit. Imitation
without improvement is defpicable, and in
the effort to give his fubjects thofe bleffings
which our neighbours derive from their fove-
reigns, it is furely much to his Majefty's glory
to have difcovered new capabilities in royalty.
That no other King dare venture fuch a deed,
is, without queftion, its brighteft eulogy!

THE fecond objection is "that an angry
" diffolution has no precedent fince the time
" of the Stewarts, that it was in fact againft
" the *fpirit* of the Conftitution. If the pre-
" rogative of diffolving Parliaments, ap-
" pointing Minifters, creating Nobles, &c.
" was to be exerted at the mere *caprice* and
" *pleafure* of the Prince, our anceftors
" would never have lodged in the chief
" Magiftrate fo monftrous an authority."
What our anceftors would *not* have done, I
know not, but I know what they *have* done.
They have lodged this power in the King—By
the

the law he has as defined a right to
appoint any Minister or diffolve any Parliament as you or I to hire or difcharge a
footman. Which of us in private life would
not deem it rank infolence, if any perfon
fhould fay, you ought to have Paul and Pe-
ter for your Cook and Butler, becaufe we
think they are good fervants. The King's
prerogative is perfectly clear and diftinct.
What has he to do with the *fpirit*, when the
letter of the law is as plain as day-light?
Has he the power?—Why is it given him?—
" Why place a barren Sceptre in his hand?"

THAT an angry diffolution has no precedent fince the revolution proves nothing but
a want of fpirit in the Princes. The fovereign's uniform acceffion to the wifh of Parliament has been our bane. We had elfe
long fince been happy, and the labour of
expofing the deformities of this Conftitution
had otherwife never refted upon me; for the
whole of the vile fabric had been humbled
with the earth before I was born. Further,
fays the *faction*, " the Empire has flourifhed
in commerce, dominion and national glory,
much beyond any other period of our annals,
fince this underftanding has prevailed between our Princes and Parliament"—Worfe
and worfe. It is not the intereft of any wife
Government, that its fubjects fhould be very
rich. Wealth begets wantonnefs, and the
judicious examples of other kingdoms de-

B 3   monftrate

monftrate the neceffity of occafional wars, famines and leffer fcourges, to ftabilitate the Government and to preferve the people in that due tone of obedience which is the certain fource of *their own content.*

So much for the clamours of the *faction*—now for the *real motives* of the diffolution. Little minds form low judgments, and narrowing the late diffolution to the meafure of fuch mean ends is very characteriftic of the groveling capacity of the Whigs ; but we are not to credit a flander which imputes to the Miniftry, fuch a fufpicious moderation. A parliament enlightened into a liberal conviction of the neceffity of fupporting the King's friends in all they fhould propofe was requifite beyond queftion, to complete this great affair. Yet was *this*, I am perfuaded, the very fmalleft motive to it. The uniform aim of the King's friends, is to open the eyes of mankind to the folly and fallacy of this Conftitution.

There is a fet of men in this country, who maintain, that the fenfe of the people can *only* be known in the Houfe of Commons : to thofe the diffolution gave a pofitive contradiction, for their fenfe *before* and *after* this event, differs as widely as light from darknefs. Another clafs there is, who contend, that the fenfe of the people never *is* nor ever *can* in its prefent fhape be collected in that Houfe. His Majefty overturned this doc-

trine

trine too, for he proclaimed his joy at the
appeal he had made to the fenfe of his people; and for the firſt time of his reign, confeſſed that his people ſpoke very good fenſe.

UNTIL the wicked principles of this
Conſtitution are as palpable as day light;
—until its numberleſs impoſtures are feen
and confeſſed—until the nation thorough-
ly underſtands the vicious ground on which
Parliaments ſtand; the annihilation of our
Parliamentary ſyſtem will not be endured;
ſhort of which we can never be a happy nation. The diſſolution went a great way to
the attainment of theſe bleſſings.

NONE of our civil quackeries is more pre-
valent than an overſtrained affectation of
purity in all the departments of our ſyſtem;
ſteeped up to the chin though we are at the
fame time in all the vileneſs of groſs corruption. It is a breach of privilege even
to *ſuppoſe* that any man fits in Parliament by
foul means—and to believe that five out of
feven get there by fair means would be con-
ſummate idiotiſm.* I am not difputing the
benefits of bribery, (its bleſſings, thank God,

B 4   are

---

* THIS Parliamentary baſhfulneſs reminds me of Henry the
Eighth. In a day or two after that good Prince beheaded
Anne Bulleyne, he began to think ſhe was innocent; and foon
after paſſed a law, making it death to *ſuſpect* the Queen's virtue. After the difcovery of Catherine Howard's irregularities
he paſſed a law, making it death to *conceal* the Queen's levities
—without repealing one word of the former law. At the fame
                                                        time

are facred and fecure) my wifh, in an humble
purfuit of the example of the Miniftry, is to
difplay the knavery of the Conftitution.

It is meet to bribe the people into a proper choice of reprefentatives for they could
otherwife never felect fit Members. Government is the moft capable of guiding the
electors in fuch a feafon of doubt, and its
good effects are manifeft from this fact, that in
the fpace of a century no Minifter has been in
a minority in a *new* Parliament. Every general
Election is fuppofed to coft Government a cou-
ple of millions, and no man denies the neceffity of this under our prefent Conftitution—but
it is a mifchievous Conftitution that impofes
fo defperate a neceffity. And I am fatisfied,
that in forcing upon the public the vaft expences of the late diffolution,---under that
immediate preffure of exigencies,---the vaft
load of debt, funded and unfunded,---the

time he paffed another law, making it high treafon for any woman to marry the King who was not *a virgin*. The King conceived himfelf fkilful in thefe diftinctions but was fometimes
miftaken, as I am told a wife man might be. The two firft laws
left his fubjects in a ftrange difficulty and the laft reduced his
wives to a fate feemingly harder (confidering that the proof
could only be a matter of opinion to all but the Lady herfelf)
Still it is a queftion, which fared worft, his male or female fubjects. Henry had no trial by jury, for that great Prince had a
good idea of things in general. He erected a tribunal of Lords,
Bifhops and Judges, and his trials never failed as the reader
will recollect. He could hang a fubject as Nero did, becaufe
his looks difpleafed him. For no better reafon perhaps, he
quieted fo many of his Queens. A refufal of marriage was
infamy and compliance was fomething more than *a chance* of
death. Utrum horum mavis accipe.

diminution

diminution of revenue,---the contraction of
refources,---the decline of credit,---the fall
of ftock, --and a national bankruptcy ftaring
us in the face, the King's friends by that ingenious expedient, meant to beget in the
people a hatred of our civil fyftem and to pre-
pare them to bear its fpeedy downfal without a figh.

A THOUSAND advantages of a lefler fize,
call for angry diflolutions of Parliament.
Election contefts would beggar the factions that oppofe the government. Expences
would difcourage, and defeats difhearten
them. Even their victories would prove
fatal. Succefs would animate them to frequent conflicts. A feries of ftruggles would
exhauft them by degrees, until convinced of
their difparity for fuch a warfare, they would
abandon the field in defpair, and leave the
King's friends peace and leifure to mould a
fit form of Government for this country, at
their own difcretion.

DISSOLUTIONS would encreafe their pow-
er---Tumults always invigorate the arm
of Government and in fuch feafons a Minifter can beft difplay his capacity. He can
raife a riot with the King's money, and quell
it with the King's army. Sober men would
be fhocked at the licence of elections and
perhaps fubmit to fervitude, to be fecured
from outrage. Good men, or men fo called,
would be difgufted with the profligacy of new
Parliaments,

Parliaments, (whofe devotion to the current Minifter is infallible) and by a frequent evidence of their turpitude, may wifh the final downfal of fuch a certain fource of vilenefs. Men of the world oppreffed by that encreafe of taxes, confequent upon fuch events, and prevented the fair produce of their avocations by confufion and diforder, would adopt any alternative in preference to fuch an evil.---Thus from the mixed effect of the indolence, the honefty, and the avarice of mankind; repeated diffolutions (timed to feafons of diftrefs and diftraction) might bring the nation into fuch a humour, that in fome lucky hour the whole fabrick of the Conftitution may be erafed to the ground.

If the Commons at any future time fhould refift the King's favorites, a hint of a diffolution is an admirable key to keep them in time. The certainty of expence, the uncertainty of fuccefs upon a frefh election, will powerfully incline them to compliance; but if *determined* to oppofe, the courfe is obvious—Raife an army of petitioners and then diffolve the Parliament. Every government can procure favourable addreffes at any time with the utmoft facility. Richard Cromwell received juft ninety addreffes as the rightful heir of the empire,—. about fix weeks before he fhrunk into nothing; and moft of the towns, counties, and corpora-

corporations in the kingdom, plighted their
loyalty, with their lives and fortunes, to James
the Second---a few months before they banifhed him.

BUT what if the people fhould decry a
future Houfe of Commons for fervility to
the Court, as they did the laft for refiftance?
Then the reigning Prince has only to look
to the conduct of George the Third, and he
will furnifh him with a mountain of precedents—" He cannot liften to their peti-
" tions, whilft his faithful Commons think
" otherwife!" The full tide of twenty-three
years practice will tell him, that the People
of England, *out* of the Houfe of Commons,
deferve juft as much notice from the Crown,
as the people of Liliput—oppofed by nothing but the miraculous inftance of 1784.

IN fhort, fo admirably does the late diffolution operate, that the King's friends can
whenever they pleafe, feparate that body
which theConftitution pretends to be infeparable, and at any time fo play the *parliament* and
people againft each other, that if the Lower
Houfe fhould not be happily demolifhed in
toto, it is reduced to a pitch of debility
and difgrace that fortunately renders it
nearly tantamount to annihilation—and fo
aufpicious is the promife from this brave
example, that the Miniftry can, even under
our prefent form of government, blefs us
with all the benefits which neighbouring
nations

nations enjoy from the lucky extinction of freedom and the judicious furrender of thefe obnoxious liberties into the hands of their Sovereigns, which are the fource of endlefs calamities to this devoted ifland.

So much for the acceffion of the prefent Miniftry to power and the meafures that fucceeded it—the diffolution and the motives to it.

HOT MEN, with eager fancies, imagine that the whole of this iniquitous parliamentary fyftem might have been deftroyed in the late ferment of the public had the King's friends been as bold as their numberlefs advantages in the ftruggle would have born them out in. That the very name of Parliament was blotted from our remembrance, is the cordial with or my heart; but I am convinced that any other courfe than the courfe adopted by the King's friends, had been to rifk this great fcheme by a rafh and over-vaulting zeal.

THE wifdom is infinite of making the impofing ceremonies of this fyftem the very inftruments of its overthrow. Parliament alone can deftroy itfelf and through that channel only can we expect the accomplifhment of this mighty undertaking. The final ruin of fo cumbrous a fyftem cannot be effected at once. The work muft be done gradually to infure fuccefs. And the reader will

find

find that the Kings friends purſued the obſject with ſkill and ſpirit and deciſion.

The Engliſh Conſtitution has veſted in the people three peculiar and marked rights, upon which they have valued themſelves more than by all their other civil poſſeſſions. Thoſe rights are: *the Liberty of the Preſs—the Trial by Jury—the Right of Repreſentation.* From the cradle to the grave we are plagued with the praiſes of theſe curſes of our ſyſtem. Pride, folly, and madneſs have, upon many occaſions, forced the people to declare they would ſooner periſh than part with either of them: nor is it ſurpriſing, for they are the three main hinges on which the machine of the Conſtitution depends. Had the King's friends, replete with all the authorities requiſite for the attempt, and in the full plenitude of power, left theſe rights untouched, I ſhould be the firſt to declare them as blind to the vices of this Conſtitution, as inſenſible to the bleſſings of a ſimple Monarchy, as their predeceſſors in office. But they have bravely vindicated themſelves from all ſuſpicion.

A lion preys not upon carcaſes: ſcorning the conqueſt of only *one* of them and ſenſible how dangerous is the eſcape of an accomplice, who might recruit and revenge the fall of a confederate, the King's friends in the ſhort ſpace of ſix weeks gallantly attacked this entire phalanx of privileges.

The

THE liberty of the preſs is a grievance of the firſt magnitude. Unleſs it be wholly aboliſhed, unleſs the wittol advocates for the Engliſh Conſtitution, are deterred from oppoſing the Miniſtry by the multitude and ſeverity of penal examples ; all hopes of ſucceſs to the GREAT CAUSE are utterly de-deluſive. Aware of its influence, the Adminiſtration made the boldeſt effort for its complete overthrow that can be found in the records of legiſlation.

THINGS were not quite mature for attacking the preſs in England, where people are ſtill under ſome infatuations in favor of it, the puſh was made in Ireland, where the enterprize was ſingularly favoured by a concurrence of circumſtances. One of the principal Miniſters, Mr. John Foſter, (a Gentleman whoſe frame of mind and tenor of principles prove, that he has right notions of the true kind of government)---brought a bill into the Iriſh Houſe of Commons, ſo remarkably well adapted to the exigency, that if paſſed into a law as the Miniſtry ſketched it out, the Iriſh, and by this time perhaps the Engliſh, would have all the benefits of the French government regarding the preſs, where a ballad cannot be publiſhed without the King's permiſſion.

To facilitate its progreſs, effectual care was taken that the moſt inflammatory and odious libels ſhould appear every day in the

ſtreets

ſtreets of Dublin, and they were circulated
through the kingdom at no ſmall expence.
The ſubſtance of one of the clauſes will ſhew
that the bill was ample and comprehenſive..

*Every Juſtice of the Peace throughout the
kingdom, ſhall be impowered to take up and com-
mit to Bridewell for ſix months, any perſon who
ſhould be found ſelling, diſperſing, circulating, or
publiſhing any advertiſement, paragraph, newſ-
paper, book, pamphlet, or publication, which he
the Juſtice ſhould deem a libel.* But alas, this
excellent clauſe was thrown out by the Committee. *Telum imbelle ſine ictu conjecit.* Our
deareſt gratitude however is due to the Miniſtry, for " what men dare, they dared ;"
all their *influence* in the ſiſter kingdom appeared in the ſupporters of this bill and all
their *ingenuity* in the title of it. What do
you think they called it ?—" *A Bill to ſecure
the Liberty of the Preſs.*" Nations are like
children and will ſwallow poiſon if gilded
with a good name. The freedom of the
preſs might be truly called the *neck* of the
Conſtitution, without which it cannot breathe,
and in this great experiment, the Miniſtry
meant to execute the famous theory of Caligu-
la, who wiſhed the Roman people had but one
neck, that he might cut them off with a *ſingle
blow.* Had this bill paſſed in its original ſtate, I
leave the reader to judge, whether the Conſtitution was not as effectually *cut off* as the
Roman

Roman people would have been, had their Emperor's pious wish been realized.

THE *second* of these rights was attacked here among ourselves, under the same gloss and colour. The Irish Chancellor of the Exchequer attempts the subversion of the liberty of the press, under the banner of " *a* " *Bill to secure it.*"—The English Chancellor of the Exchequer atchieves the overthrow of the *trial by jury,* and at the same moment extols the trial by jury to the skies. This second right the reader must know, has been held so sacred and precious by our abfurd ancestors, that it has been the first privilege they demanded of their Kings after the various changes of our government in the early ages of our history. The religion of the people impressed not a warmer love of the Deity, than their civil code taught reverence for this very right. Yet such is the progress of improvement upon our minds, so rapidly are our bigotries vanishing, so quick are the strides of conviction upon our understanding, and so generally enlightened are we become, that this trial by Jury has been given up (bating some factious opposition in the House of Commons) with as little concern and as profound an indifference by the body of the public, as if it had been an inclosure bill.

BUT

BUT were juries annihilated in the trial of offences committed in England?—No!—It only related to our poſleſſions in India, where more crimes are perpetrated in ſeven days, than in the reſt of the Empire in ſeven years.

THE third is the *right of repreſentation*.

THE *very firſt* proceeding of the new parliament proves, that the people really have no ſuch right, and promotes THE CAUSE as deciſively as if the cuſtom of calling parliaments was laid aſide altogether. The Weſtminſter ſcrutiny (the proceeding to which I allude) is pregnant with a thouſand advantages. The King calls a Houſe of Commons for the diſpatch of urgent concerns upon a fixed day. To diſpatch theſe concerns they muſt *meet*. Now meet they cannot, for the returning officer will not ſuffer them. Why?—Becauſe he cannot tell which is the greater number, *two* or *one*. What then is to become of the *urgent concerns?*—No matter. This determination you obſerve, as to law and principle, is tantamount to the poſitive denial of this *right of repreſentation*. But the great virtue of the deciſion conſiſts in its overturning doctrines by wholeſale, which have been reverenced for ages in this wicked conſtitution. It proves that the people may be bound by laws *not of their own making*: That they muſt pay taxes to which *they did not conſent*. It makes election a farce, and a popular choice the means of having no choice

C   at

at all. The King's friends went far to ferve us in the Middlefex cafe, but the obftacle is prodigious if the *return of members be once made.* Wilkes's character was the chief incitement to that feat, but we loft the ufe of the precedent, for the univerfe could not produce Wilkes's match. The *manner* of the thing was vile, but here it was admirable.—The *candidate of the court* has only to tell the *officer of the court*, that his adverfary had bad votes, and the whole is done at once. *This is the law of England,* and the principle is univerfal in its operation, whether the cafe be Weftminfter or Weft Loo.

But, fay the enemy,—" This decifion is " a direct violation of law, conftitution, juf- " tice, equity, reafon, and common fenfe— " it is a direct breach of the ftatute of Ed- " ward III. Henry VI. William III. and in " all the law books, records of parliaments, " reports, cafes, compilations; in fhort from " the foundation of our hiftory, *not one pre-* " *cedent* can be found for this bafe decifion." To all this I anfwer, fo much the better. Scruples about laws and mufty precedents would little become the King's friends, lifted to the pinnacle of authority.* That would have been as if Oliver Cromwell had not cut off the King's head, after fweating at every pore to have the power of doing it.

---

* The fame rapid and decifive fpirit was fhewn upon the Bedfordfhire queftion.

OTHER

Other motives are attributed to this decifion. The exclufion of Fox from Weftminfter, and a zeal to opprefs him, are faid to be
the chief inducements. Private rancour and
perfonal revenge are undoubtedly very laudable incitements to a public meafure, and
admitting that the King's friends had not defigns more dignified, and aims more enlarged
—granting for argument, that the Weftminfter fcrutiny was not meant as an inftrument
of our deliverance from this pernicious conftitution, I am convinced that even thofe
vulgar views which are imputed to the miniftry carry with them an unanfwerable vindication.

It has been the very extremity of infolence
in Fox to fit for Weftminfter, in defiance of
the King's friends ! the firft city of the kingdom ! the feat of empire ! the fountain of
authority ! in the heart of which, his majefty expends about a million a year ! Thefe
confiderations are ferious; but the fuccefs of
this daring man was of a tenfold mortification in the late conteft.—It falfified the af-
fertions of his unpopularity, when every
quill that worked for the miniftry, was died
in gall to blacken him. The mifchief was
greater ftill, for this inference followed—
that where *he* and *his enemies* were *beft known,*
the balance of public claim was as much in
his favour, as it was in *their favor* where *each
were perfonally ftrangers* and where a line of
unadulterated fact fcarce ever reaches. The

C 2   current

current opinion of minifterial impofture and public infanity, were greatly ftrengthened by it without difpute.

But there is another light in which this fcrutiny is compleatly juftified. Impatience under defeat is natural, and the genius of human nature kicks againft a rival's fuperiority in any thing. Great men, they fay, are moved by great events—boys by trifles. Not content with having a majority upon the Weftminfter election, Fox *would have a triumph*, in the manner of which, the impudence of the *faction* exceeded all decency. As if their only aim was to fatirize the minifter's vifit to the city, the whole proceffion feemed an infult and perfonal mortification to him, and by their own picture, (which I fhall give the reader) the refentment of the court will appear wife and proper.

" Whatever this country contains of high nobility, ancient blood, rank, reputation and fortune,—whatever it boafts of fplendid inheritance, titles that dignify, becaufe they were deferved, and virtue unqueftioned from a variety of trials.—Whatever has elevated, and ftill retains us in characters of refpect, diftinction, and fame with other nations.—All that fhine moft eminent and reflect glory and grace upon their country, in arts, arms, fcience, learning, ability.—The great, who are truly fo becaufe they are good, the little, who are refpectable becaufe they are independent.—Men in humble walks,
who

who affert the native dignity of Englifhmen,
by an unbought adherence to the object of
their choice—men in high ftations, whofe
conduct infpires, whofe manners cherifh that
fentiment, and whofe cordial intercourfe with
thofe placed by fortune far below them, en-
courage and fortify that fyftem of principles
which impart an equal blefling to the peer
and the peafant.—The nobleft names in
Englifh hiftory, Howards, Cavendifh's, Ben-
tincks, Spencers, Stanleys, Fitzwilliams, &c.
thofe whofe anceftors lavifhed their blood
and property in defending this country from
foreign enemies, and native traitors, who
under various ftruggles, from various caufes,
refcued the nation from oceans of perils, into
opulence, fecurity, and renown.—Even they
who depend for their ftations upon the fovereign's will (the officers of his own guards,
as if their mafter's livery blufhed fomething
hoftile to the firft duties of an Englifhman)
changed their ftandard upon this day, and
funk the foldier in the citizen *at all its ha-
zards.* Thus conftituted was this proceffion,
and fuch are the men who boafted loyalty to
fuch a leader.

" AND if yet higher the proud lift fhould
    end."—

IF any thing was yet wanting to compleat its fplendor—The firft fubject of the
realm flufhed with joy in fuch a caufe, bore
his part with eagernefs, and thought his great

character

character still more exalted, in fanning that generous flame, that raised his own illustrious family to the glory of governing such a people."

I HAVE given this picture as the faction paint it. Heightened it is without doubt, but still the subject was a reasonable ground of noble and just jealousy in our matchless minister, whose notable cavalcade to Grocers-hall, becomes, upon review of both, the meerest burlesque that ever damped the pride of young ambition. The scene, the circumstance, the champions render a comparison inevitable. Alas!—our cousins of *Buckingham* and *Mahon*.---*Sidney* the sapient and candid *Camelford!* * a city job with John Wilkes! and a chosen troop of active infantry (to illume the darkened domes of senseless Westminster at night) who scoured the shops at their return, as nimble as Falstaff's battalion scoured the hedges in his memorable march to Coventry!

EVEN *this* view of things justifies the scrutiny—all my dread is, that its issue will not answer. The choice of the bailiff's *council* was a fatal mistake. Is a man bigotted to truth from principle, to rectitude from sentiment, to genius from sympathy,—disqualified by acute feelings, with as sharp a sense of honor, and a conscience of his own

as

---

* THESE comprised the retinue of Mr. Pitt to Grocers-hall.

as clear and unblemifhed, as if he had never
opened his lips to the keeper of the King's
confcience, or had never guided the confcience of the King's High Bailiff---fit for
fuch a bufinefs ?---FRANCIS HARGRAVE the
director of *Mr. Thomas Corbett!* This I fear
was an irreparable flip.*

No people ever reached the bleffings of
flavery without their own co-operation. In
a complex form, like ours, this GREAT
CAUSE cannot be promoted without a confederacy of perfons high in the people's
efteem. The favorite faction in this country
has generally been the Whig faction. To
thefe, the King's friends have occafionally
dealt out the public adminiftration, but always managed their duration in office with fo
nice an œconomy, that in the twenty-five
yearsof thisprofperous reign, the *longeft* Whig
adminiftration has barely exceeded *one year*,
though they were four times employed. The
King found the government in their hands
upon his acceffion---but he foon difmiffed
their chief (Lord Chatham) and the reft
followed him. The next was Lord
Rockingham (begun in July 1765 ended
in July 1766) The third in 1782 (commenced in March, perifhed in July.) The

* THE agents of the miniftry have lately made a moft bold
and frontlefs pufh to get rid of Mr. Hargrave, and they will
certainly fucceed.

C 4   laft laſt in 1783 (born in April, died in December.) From all theſe exploſions the King's friends gathered up *ſome* fragments which ſtrengthened their own building---But all their former acquirements are nothing compared with the diamonds they picked up in the laſt of theſe wrecks. Lord North's coalition with Mr. Fox *had infallibly ſunk this iſland in the ocean,* if the grace of Heaven had not ſent *Pitt* to ſave us ! A mortal Meſſiah ! the miſſionary of Providence ! the light of lights ! the ſun of ſuns ! the fountain of lumination ! the choſen gift of God !---Not the Maid of Orleans to the French, not the Maid of Kent to the Engliſh, not Beckett to Bigots, not Mahomet to Ottomans, not Jack of Leyden to Anabaptiſts, not the Regal touch or Papal toe to infidelity and infection, were half ſo holy, half ſo healing, half ſo divine, as William Pitt to this nation !

Nil oriturum alias, nil ortum tale fatentes.

In Egypt he had ranked with Seſoſtris, in China with Confucius. Hecatombs had bled for him in Greece, and temples ſprung up for him in Rome. Socrates had no wiſdom, Seneca no morals, Cicero no eloquence, Cæſar no ſpirit, Sinon no cunning, Achilles no ſtrength, Ulyſſes no craft, compared to him. Modern miniſters melted before him, like ſhadows before the ſun. The genius of Fox, the judgment of Vergennes, the experience

rience of Kaunitz, fhrunk befide his matchlefs merit. All that Europe boafts, except himfelf, were dupes and drivellers. The fimplicity of the ancient, the refinement of the modern world---the capacity of elder, the ingenuity of latter times---the amiablenefs of the golden, the burnifh of the brazen, the apathy of the iron age, all centered in his fweet perfon. He was not only faultlefs in his conduct, but without a faulty particle in his nature.---Not only inimitable, but infallible. He had not *all* the qualities of the Trinity, but he fell little fhort of them.—He was a boy with an angel's faculties and a man with the attributes of a divinity. He was liftened to like an oracle. All other doctrines were apocryphal, and his were holy writ. His opinion was law, his nod judgment, his word fate.---In fhort, if Charles Jenkinfon had fat at the right hand of Jove, with the full command of both his urns, not a change would he have made in William Pitt, or in the Englifh nation---

I NEED not tell the reader the value of fuch an ally to the King's friends, and to do them juftice, they made the moft of him. If in the compafs of the one year he be not worn threadbare, it is, a miracle. As prodigal of his own character as of the conftitution, he was the firft in all the breaches of this tottering fyftem, and urged his bold career with an intrepid contempt for every confideration.

But

But was all this adoration on the youth's own account you would afk—O no—much for himfelf but more for his father. Pater *et* filius *patre dignus* ; and this is the more remarkable as for the twelve years that preceded his father's death, the nation left him withering in obfcurity, nor ever once enquired why he lay mouldering ;

" But ftill the crowd have kindnefs in referve ;
" They help'd to *bury* whom they help'd to *ftarve.*"

It is not *our* bufinefs however, who fee with open eyes the vicious deformities of this conftitution to fcrutinize the fources of our emancipation, provided we are relieved. Whether Pitt's popularity was the effeE of fober reafon or of infanity is indifferent to us, if the King's friends have turned it to a proper account.— That they have done fo, the reader perhaps may think from what he *has* read— what he has *to* read will leave no doubt of it.

MR. PITT's LIFE has been a fhort one, and previous to his late exaltation, has afforded very little to make a fixed impreffion. The chief diftinEions of his political charaEter have been thefe—*that he begun his career as a Whig—that he was an enemy to the influence of the Crown—that he detefted political corruption— that he was devoted to parliamentary reform.*

A DERE-

A DERELICTION of all his profeffions and principles upon thefe feveral points is urged againft him by the oppofition as a *crime* ; but in reality it is the effence of minifterial virtue. Tenacities for confiftency, delicacy upon the fcore of principle, the fear of infamy from running counter to the whole tenor of his recorded declarations, had all been fatal obftacles to the fuccefs of the GREAT CAUSE. Luckily however there are no fuch obftacles, and in fhewing that his enemy's reproaches are in this inftance well founded, the reader will underftand that I am bearing teftimony to fome of the nobleft features in this illuftrious young man's character, and proving his right to *our* affections and confidence.

THAT he commenced a Whig is doubtlefs. But I leave the reader to judge, whether Sir William Dolben might not juft as well be accufed of copying the model of John Hampden, as William Pitt of Whiggifm at this time.—That he was a profeffed enemy to the influence of the Crown is doubtlefs likewife. Let the *India Bill* affert his converfion from that coarfe way of thinking.---

THE third charge fuppofes him hoftile to corruption. If bribery required vindication, my labours fhould not be wanting to difplay its merits. The caufe could profper in *no degree* unaided by this beft of powers, and to impute to Mr. Pitt any enmity againft it, would be juft as reafonable as charging *Hill* with wit, or *Rolle* with good manners. The

annals

annals of the world cannot furpafs his prefent
Majefty's reign in the boundlefs exercife of
this firft of virtues, and yet all its varied and
multitudinous atchievements fall fhort of the
fingle month of January 1784. Then it was
that the reveries of a great poet became actually realized :

" Hear her black trumpet through the land
        proclaim,
" That *not to be corrupted* was the fhame."

IT was always the fafhion in *town*. At
that time, however, it became the only re-
commendation in the *country* (as the new
elections confirmed) and in working this
fufceptibility of the fenate Sir Robert Walpole himfelf was a fimpleton to this wonderful young man. There was fuch originality,
fuch ingenuity, fuch orientality in the manner.—Sources were difcovered fo unthought
of in all former exigencies—channels of influence fo myfterious and unfufpected—fluices
of venality fo contrary to all imagining---fuch
dexterity of feducement ! fuch rare and refined profligacy ! fuch polifhed proftitution !
In a word it was the ne plus ultra of this
admirable fcience !

THE laft of thefe accufations relates to
the parliamentary reform. Sunk into contempt, as they have been, I hope no event
will ever happen by which the commons
will dare to affume any influence in the fcale
                                                    of

of this government. A *meliorated* * reform, that is to fay, a reform which fhould leave the Houfe of Commons as much at the minifter's devotion as it is at this moment, nay, if well managed, ftill more fubfervient than it is, might be a good bugbear to the people (whofe aid in their own redemption from this noxious conftitution is indifpenfible) and by the help of Mr. Wyvill's letters, which of courfe will affure the reformers in the country, that Pitt's fcheme is the *beft of all fchemes*, might produce folid benefit to the miniftry—but the experiment is hazardous after all. The leaft tafte of reform may en-creafe the public appetite for more, and no-thing *can* be ventured that might rifk the refurrection of the lower houfe.

The firft and fafteft impreffion Mr. Pitt made upon his country has been by the re-form of parliament. He figured in it with a moft bewitching gallantry, and appeared as earneft in promoting it, as Cæfar in fup-preffing Cataline's plot. Twice in two years he has been in power, and all we heard from him touching the reform, during his mi-niftry, was taunting thofe who brought it forward with envy and malice, or pouring fhowers of invective upon Lord North, *for*

---

* Mr. Wyvill's notable letter to the Secretary of the Edin-rough Committee fays, that Mr. Pitt will now fupport a re-form *honeftly* and *boldly*, which by the way does *not* imply that his fupport of it hitherto has been deceit and knavery. Whe-ther Pitt's aim is to repair his popularity by a *ferious* hypo-crify, or to terrify his mafters, a few weeks will develope. Either object is worthy of him.

fear

fear his lordſhip ſhould freeze in his long declared oppoſition to that ſcheme. But the moment his miniſtry ceaſed, he relapſed back into the reform fever, and boiled and bubbled for its ſucceſs, with as much ardour and inflammation as Henry Dundas himſelf, who is miraculouſly become a convert to this ſyſtem, and like all converts, *is mad* for his new faith.

But John Bull (an animal of eternal good cheer) is conſoled with the certainty of the miniſter's bringing forward the reform in perſon—He *will* indeed bring it forward, and the love I bear him forces me to beſpeak the public notice to the miniſter-like qualities he will diſplay on the occaſion. He carried the Weſtminſter ſcrutiny, it is true, and it is true that his *dead* majority is 200. *But the reform is a buſineſs upon which men will think for themſelves.* Mr. Wilberforce will be brilliant in praiſe of his honourable friend's *ſincerity*, and another dinner in Downing-ſtreet, may procure another pithy panegyric from

---

* This requires explanation. Alderman Sawbridge in the month of July, called upon the miniſter to bring forward the reform. The miniſter ſat ſilent—The alderman ſaid, as the miniſter would not bring it forward, *he* would, and gave a week's notice to the houſe of his motion.—When the day came ſeveral profeſſed friends of the reform, and of the miniſter, begged he would poſtpone the motion for a few days, and urged the unfitneſs of that ſeaſon to try the queſtion. The alderman delayed the motion for another week, but contended that the time preſent was of all other the very beſt. ' The reform was ' popular—the parliament was come hot from the people—the ' miniſter was pledged to the meaſure. The Weſtminſter ſcru-' tiny proved that the houſe would go with him any length *when*

from Mr. Milnes. * In fhort, Pitt will *propofe*
it—Pitt's friends will *reject* it—he will get
rid of the bufinefs with a moft technical
eclat, and the whole nation *will be convinced,*
that the reform is loft fimply and certainly,
becaufe he cannot help it.

So much for *fpeculation,* now for *fact.* Let
us crofs the channel and behold our young
minifter combat this reform in the fifter kingdom. I pafs by his anfwer to the chairman
of the Belfaft meeting. A letter which only
proves, that in Jefuitifm even *Shelburne* was
a *Shippen* to him, is beneath notice, when
events of the rareft celebrity call forth our
wonder.

THAT fpecies of polity which does not
fcruple to cover nations with mifery for the
promotion of its own objects, (although reprobated by weak nerved people, as crooked
and infamous) is the perfection of a ftatefman. Not into Machiavel would I look for
its vindication, but into the heart of man,
and the genius of human nature. Whilft

---

* *when he really wifhed it :* all thefe advantages he was deter-
* mined not to forego.'---Mr. Milnes (the member for York)
in a private converfation with Mr. Sawbridge, applauded his
perfeverance, and urged him not to yield again to delay the
motion on any terms, for that all the objections to it were farcical. In a few days after, when he made the motion, the
friends of the miniftry again contended, that the time was un-
feafonable, and great was the alderman's furprife to find *this
very Mr. Milnes* moft clamorous in the fame opinion. This
fudden change of fentiment is, however, accounted for when
the reader hears, that *Mr. Milnes dined with Mr. Pitt at the
Treafury houfe in Downing-ftreet, a day or two before the motion
was made.*

Lewis

Lewis IV. was flaughtering the proteftants of France, he paid the proteftants of Germany for maintaining their faith to the laft gafp, in defiance of the Emperor, who was at the fame time fertilizing his dominions with the blood of *his* proteftant fubjects. .

WHILST the chambers of the Spanifh inquifition were perfuming with the daily incenfe of heretical facrifice, Philip's minifters animated the French heretics with money, and every other means of diftracting their country, and of goading their Sovereign into the fatal meafure to him and to themfelves, of revoking the edict of Nantz. In thefe policies there was undoubted virtue ! But what is their virtue compared with William Pitt's method of overturning the reform of parliament in Ireland ?

THOSE were rival nations, eager and determined on the ruin of each other.

BUT for the governing minifter to raife, or ftrive to raife, an infurrection among the governed, purely to prevent the fuccefs of a fyftem, which fyftem that very minifter was folemnly pledged to promote, conftitutes an event fo new in civil fcience, and forms a political feature fo fuper-excellent, that as it ftands without a parallel in paft times, it may be fairly faid to defie the reach of future imitation.

THAT a civil war did not enfue, diminifhes in no fenfe the merit of the miniftry. All that defperate ingenuity, and a brave contempt

tempt of confequences could do, they did.
The Irifh furrendered all other difcontents:—
not a heart panted, not a wifh was uttered for
any object *but a reform of parliament.* Great
was the difeafe, but the remedy was greater.
In the effort to fet religion againft religion,
and by that means to fet father againft fon,
brother againft brother, and friend againft
friend; the miniftry provoked the revival of
the moft effectual of all animofities.—That
which defolated Europe for two centuries,
and had been at all times moft fatal to the
repofe of mankind, could not fail to deftroy
the reform, becaufe it muft *divide the people* *.

TRUST and confidence between large bodies
of fubjects is always injurious to the *power*
of government, and independent of fubverting the reform by it, the policy was admirable of infufing the feeds of feparation and
difcord among the Irifh.

BUT the comprehenfive foul of the minifter grafped ftill more. " I will conquer
America in *Germany*," faid the Earl of Chatham—I will cut up the *Englifh reform* in *Ireland!* fays the Earl of Chatham's fon †. In
the

* See the addreffes carried in Ireland by the miniftry and
their anfwers, through the Duke of Rutland, where a danger
of fubverting the proteftant eftablifhment is dextroufly ftarted
*when the moft cordial union fubfifted between all the religions in
that kingdom.*

† Whatever be the reader's political complexion, I befeech,
I *implore* him, to read the publifhed fpeech of Mr. Pitt's newly
made

the profecution of thofe who called meetings
in Ireland, the worthy youth ftrikes at the
foundation of thofe affemblies in England
that ftill keep alive this phrenzy of reform;
—affemblies that have in times paft honoured himfelf upon this fubject, but which, by
the way, is a very ftatefmanlike reafon for
defpifing them at prefent.

THE fkill of man can conceive nothing

made Chief Juftice of the Irifh King's-bench, Lord Earlsfort,
where he will find thefe precious points affirmed to be the law of
the land, not by quirk or fubtlety, but in home fpun intelligible
terms.—1ft. " *That the power of the county is the power of the
crown*."—2d. That the Sheriffs calling the people together
peacefully and legally, " *is the moft wanton oppreffion of the
King's fubjects*."—3d. " *That a reformation of parliament is, as
plain as words can fpeak, to overturn the religion and confitu-
tion of their country*." 4th. That *attachments* are prefer-
able to *trials*, becaufe they are fummary, becaufe *the whole
county is corrupted*, and no *jury fhould be trufted*—5th. (which
is a moft holy doctrine, and the eccho of the Britifh plan in
deftroying the trial by jury) that a trial by jury of fuch charges
would be highly improper, " *becaufe it would be running the
hazard of corrupting witneffes*, and TEMPTING A JURY TO
PERJURE THEMSELVES." Here you fee the foundation of this
vaunted trial is fubverted, root and branch,—for in every human litigation, there is a rifk of perjury.

I know that conftitutionalifts may fay this: If the publifhed fpeech of the Irifh Judge be fpurious, *the publifher
fhould lofe his ears*—If it be genuine, the Judge *fhould lofe
his life*. The criminal juftice of the country is endangered
every hour that fuch a traitor to the conftitution pollutes
the bench; and the people, if they do not impeach him,
are madmen, flaves, or cowards.—I am of a very different opinion, and it is a fubftantial caufe of delight for *us* to reflect,
that though the *Britifh* bench is barren of *fuch* characters, the
miniftry have bleffed the *Irifh* with a Judge, who comprehends
in his own perfon, the nobleft faculties of a *Trefilian*, a *Scroggs*,
a *Bacon*, and a *Jefferies*.

more

more exquifite than the policy of government in the affairs of Ireland. Befide the
outrages fo feafonably perpetrated in that
country, they have contrived that the moft
frantic theories fhould be difperfed there,
which enable them to propagate on this fide
of the water, that the Irifh mean nothing
fhort of *entire feparation.* A cordiality between the two kingdoms had been fatal.—
In that cafe nothing *could* prevent the fuccefs
of the reform. The miniftry have therefore
moft wifely fent forth this judicious calumny, to obviate all *fellow feeling,* and their ma-
nœuvres are luckily affifted by the moft drunk-
en ftupidity on the part of the reformers
themfelves, both in Ireland and England.

SOME men will remark, no doubt, that
the Irifh (after cafting away all other com-
plaints and converging the whole of their
grievances in *that fingle* point,) will, if *they
relinquifh the reform,* be the bafeft and vileft
band of daftardly cowards that ever rendered
a nation infamous.—It may be fo, but that
is no bufinefs of ours. If the minifter fubdues
the reform *radically* in that kingdom, *our*
boundlefs gratitude is due to him.

SINCE WE ARE YET conftrained to endure the evil of parliamentary legiflation, the
next enquiry is, whether Mr. Pitt has profited
of the public idolatry. If he has been a nig-
gard in the ufes of his fortune, and betrayed a

pufi-

pufilanimous moderation in the limitlefs power his good ftars conferred upon him, it were undoubtedly criminal; but you will find he ftands as guiltlefs of this imputation, as Scylla did when he became Dictator, and purified the ftreets of Rome with the blood of thofe who made him fo.

Throughout the feffions, the minifter kept his eye fteadily upon the cause. Whatever is moft hoftile to the principles of this conftitution, is traced and eftablifhed in almoft every meafure he has introduced.

Our fyftem of government inculcates good faith, and at the fame, a due œconomy towards the public creditors. The minifter fubverted the firft in his conduct upon the *Navy bills,* and the fecond upon the *Ordinance debentures.* Public faith and public œconomy were fpiritedly abandoned in both tranfactions. The taxes he has impofed, may, with truth, be called a compendium of *all* that is obnoxious to conftitutional doctrines.— " Though all the winds of heaven fhould " enter the ragged cabin of the pooreft pea- " fant—the King fhall not, the King dare " not enter it,"—faid the Earl of Chatham, in a fpeech reprobating *excife laws.* The meaneft knave that cheats the public, to cheat the King, as an excife officer, not only *dares,* but *fhall* enter and fearch, not merely every houfe, but every crevice of it, if he choofe,

choofe, fays the Earl of Chatham's fon, in the fubftance of a fpeech *eftablifhing* excife laws.

THE *game acts* have generally been deemed a fpecies of *foreft laws*. Now, Mr. Pitt's game act has *no other* operation than nerving thofe laws with new energy. As a fource of revenue it is long given up, but it poffeffes this mark of a great capacity, that all the fkill of the kingdom combined, is unequal to its comprehenfion.—Too fubtle and fublime for vulgar underftandings, the only meaning on the face of it confifts in ftimulating men to perfecute each other, by an unexampled encouragement to informers.

THE *commutation tax* is the burthen of every exclamation from Penzance to the Orkneys, and in that long diftrict we are told there is but one opinion upon it (except at the Treafury and in Leadenhall-ftreet.) I will not combat prejudice, but of this I am fatisfied, that there is in the commutation tax fomething better for *us* than the beft tax ever impofed by the beft of men in the beft of times,—perfuading myfelf that our redemption from this curfed conftitution, depends chiefly on the duration of the prefent minifter's power and popularity, and feeling, convinced, that the man who laid *this tax*, and ftill continues (without much diminution of public or parliamentary influence) to be the finance minifter of this country, may now with perfect fafety attempt *any thing*.

THE

THE affair of the *fix regiments* fhews fomething fo characteriftic of the miniftry and fo aufpicious to *the caufe*, that I muft bring it to the reader's recollection.

KINGS love money and territory, but they love the army ftill better—becaufe an army will never want bread whilft they wear bayonets, and in any ftruggle between the Monarch and his fubjects their arguments are wonderous convincing. The emancipation of kingdoms from liberty to fervitude has feldom been atchieved without them, and hence the love of Princes, and the jealoufy of free States for ftanding armies. Our filly conftitution is fo fcrupulous on this head that we never vote a foldier, nor the money that pays him, nor the law that binds him, for more than one year. The *lower* a Minifter reduced the military, the frowns of the crown, or the favours of the people have in common calculation been *proportionably* dealt to him, and the choice of his patron of courfe depended on his own difcretion.

THE bufinefs before us will throw a ftrong light upon the late adminiftration, and prove their arrogance in daring to prefume that they poffeffed one fpark of the honeft confidence of George the Third.

THE firft peace eftablifhment of this reign was fixed under Lord Bute in 1763, at 70 regiments, each confifting of ten companies.

The

The fecond was in 1783, under the Duke of Portland, when the regiments were fixed at *fixty-four*, with only *eight* companies in each. By this laft eftablifhment the whigs would impudently deprive his majefty of *fix regiments* together with 140 companies, and deprive the nation the pleafure of paying for them. Thus ftood the arrangement when the King, to his eternal honour, difmiffed the whigs.

MANY things there are very defirable to be done, which expedience prohibits. To fix the army upon the plan of Lord Bute in 1763, was an object devoutly to be wifhed, but it were an attempt of great delicacy. All that the matchlefs youth could fafely do, he did. Since he could not directly reftore the old eftablifhment, he reviled thofe who reduced it, and heartily eafed himfelf of three or four lufty fits of invective againft the whigs upon the occafion, loudly queftioned their fincerity in lefiening the national expences, and fo forth.

OF the officers of the regiments reduced by this arrangement many had purchafed at advanced prices, prefuming that they would not be reduced at the peace. Their cafe was confidered by the Houfe of Commons a hard one, and the whig Secretaries of State* and of the war department faid, they certainly

* MESSRS. Fox and Fitzpatrick.

in-

intended to provide for them. The provision was, to *second* them upon the army in general, and allow them full pay until they were promoted; employing them in the mean while upon the recruiting service. Their own regiments were of course to be disbanded. This method was very unpalateable to the King's friends, for two excellent reasons,—because the *military should not be reduced* on any terms, and because *seconding* these officers *deprived them of the army patronage*, until these officers were provided for.

THE Ministry consulted for several days upon the business. At length their sagacious Secretary at War informed the House of Commons, that the officers would be completly satisfied if they were allowed full pay for six months longer, and he accordingly moved the money. Upon an official declaration that full pay for *six months* would *compleatly satisfy* those, who expected it *for life* the House had only to wonder. The House did wonder greatly, but not half so much as upon hearing in a day or two after, by authority of the officers themselves, that in the Secretary's *official information, there was not one syllable of truth.* Suffice it to tell the reader, that the present Ministry adopted a course the direct reverse of their predecessors. They have *preserved the army patronage compleat* to themselves.—Not one of the officers

officers is to be *feconded.*—The nation pays for the whole body *(for the fake of giving full pay to the officers)* and *the fix entire regiments are ready for any exigency at the call of the King's friends.* Yet there *are* men who affect to wonder at the steps which the beft of Kings has taken to overthrow the whigs !

THOSE WHO THINK as I do of the Englifh conftitution (and to thofe alone I write) muft fee the intrinfic excellence of all Mr. Pitt's meafures in the laft feffions, but his *manner* enhances his merit confiderably. Hitherto the prefumption has been, that when a plan is folemnly propofed by a Minifter of State, it is deliberately confidered, digefted with fkill, and enriched with the various informations acceffible to government. But in this method there are two leading defects—firft it muft be very troublefome to the minifter—fecondly, it is treating Parliament with a refpect utterly repugnant to the promotion of THE CAUSE.

THESE defects were admirably remedied by Mr. Pitt. Excepting where the conftitution was aimed at, his meafures *going out of*, and *coming into*, the Houfe of Commons have not the fainteft trace of fimilitude. They *become* radically and folidly the reverfe of what they *have been.* But was not all this conceffion, good humour, facility, accommodation ? --- O fie, no. Such difpofitions were fatal to us.

HE

He propofes a fpecific plan upon a fpecific day. The genius of man can conceive nothing more perfect, and he is refolved not to abandon one principle. In debate it appears not quite fo perfect---it turns out a heap of nonfenfe, and in a few days after he brings it down transformed into a new fhape. Nothing can equal the *new fhape*: he cannot be perfuaded to alter a line, and he gallantly taunts its oppofers for ignorance and abfurdity. A frefh difcuffion fhews frefh deformities. The *fame* plan comes again a week after perhaps, in *another* form, as diftant from the fecond as the fecond from the firft. An equal loftinefs and contempt of the enemy accompany the third *entre*, and at length it is carried off the ftage in all the flafh of triumph---differing as widely from its original nature, as Pitt the fon from Pitt the father.

These inftances of fuperior capacity occurred I believe upon every *great* occafion throughout the feffions.

NOTHING HAS YET BEEN SAID of the India Company in the courfe of this pamphlet, for it were indecent to degrade them by blending their affairs with meaner matter. The majefty of the fubject oppreffes me, and I am really at a lofs in what point of view firft to contemplate them---whether as

men

men who, when our empire in Europe was
abridging, exterminated whole nations in
Afia, purely to extend our dominions---or as
men who, when our military fame had been
declining, fwept off millions of the human
race without any other impulfe than the generous wifh of preferving fome balance of
our reputation, and proving that Englifh
heroifm flourifhed in India beyond the moft
vigorous examples in our hiftory---or as men
who, when we were finking into a medi-
ocrity of character, afferted our native energy
in a feries of judicious perfecutions, provi-
dent oppreffions, and the moft wife and well-
managed barbarities---or as men who, when
we were weakening at home into a conceit-
ed reverence of treaties with other nations,
nobly redeemed us from fuch unbecoming
fcruples by a fpirited and gallant contempt
of all ties, agreements, and engagements
whatfoever---or as men who, when our government here became languid and paffive,
and fuffered its fubjects to remonftrate, counteract, and expoftulate upon all occafions,
gaveu s fpecimens of the true genius of
found policy by defolating kingdoms, expel-
ling tributary princes like vagabonds, and
feizing upon their *all*, for daring to plead
the fanction of covenants and the right of
treaties folemnly ratified---or as men, who
when we were withering into obfcurity and
finking

sinking in the notice we formerly maintained through Europe, made our power so intelligible, our character so notorious, and our name so tremendous, that not an Indian through the unmeasured wilds of Asia ever addresses his God without mixing *Englishmen* in his prayer ---or as men who impoverished whole kingdoms, not for the sordid sake of personal lucre, but the patriot zeal of enriching their native country---who imported enormous wealth, not for a vicious waste of it, not to disgust us by their prodigality, nor offend by their insolence, but to improve us by their good manners, their moderation and morality---and who (as the best benefit they could render the English nation) when we were degenerating back into the gloominess, the moroseness and barbarism of the last age, gave a fillip to expiring luxury, and dimmed the brilliancy of our noblest families by superior splendour and magnificence.

In all these views the India Company challenge our admiration, but even this mass of virtues is slight in the scale of their conduct towards the present ministry in the late struggle.

Limited to space, and constrained by time, I cannot here detail their numberless friendships,

" What seas they traversed, and what
    " fields they fought."

Their

'Their influence, their power, their purfe, were devoted to the King's friends. All their diligence, all their ingenuity, all their experience, were exerted. Every other care was caſt aſide. Schemes of conqueſt and depredation were ſuſpended. Their own defence was given up for the defence of the miniſtry. Fraud, rapine, and robbery were left to ſhift for themſelves—even Haſtings was forgot. Every lung was diſtended, every voice clamorous for the matchleſs miniſter. Their orators were hoarſe in his praiſe — their authors periſhing in his panegyric. Language was beggared for him. Epithets and inkſtands run dry, and not a quiet hour did they enjoy until the adminiſtration was out of all danger. In return, the miniſtry were truly grateful, for between them and the Company, nothing occurred through the ſeſſions, but mutual conceſſion and reciprocity of good offices.

Both had but one object, with different views. The Company wiſhed to ſtand upon their old footing, the miniſtry wiſhed to prove the late adminiſtration a ſet of liars, and the late parliament a band of libellers.—Two Committees had, in the courſe of three years, formed a mountain of reports. The amount of them was, that the government of the India Company in Europe, was the moſt prepoſterous and deſpicable that could be imagined, pernicious to the intereſts, and fatal to the

the honour of this nation.—That the government in India was a fyftem of uniform dif-obedience, and ftudied contempt of the Company, executed for the fole purpofe of en-riching the fervants, which enabled them to fcoff at their mafters, and defy all the law, juftice and power of this country,—which riches were derived from barefaced extortion, violence, perfidy, oppreffion, and cruelty, upon the miferable natives of that devoted country. This was the fum of the Reports.—Mr. Pitt's India Bill confirmed the whole of them to be a mafs of impudent calumny, it proved that the government at home was truly a wife one, and the fervants abroad a very honeft fet of gentlemen.

THE different relief bills went upon the fame principle. Fox faid the Company were in a ftate of bankruptcy—Pitt adopted the moft infallible means of falfifying Fox. He gives the Company a boundlefs ufe of their credit (which the nation deprived them of, to prevent a repetition of the South Sea bubble.) He forgives them for one year, the payment of above nine hundred thoufand pounds (without any charge of intereft.) The Company turned this fum to their own purpofes, and the finking fund was deficient to that exact amount. To fupply the finking fund, he borrows the entire fum at 5 ¼ per cent. —with a moft generous gratitude he charges the

the nation *fifty four thousand pounds a year; for lending the nation's own money to the India Company*, and then paffes a law to allow them to divide 8 per cent. *(the largeft dividend they ever made in their moft profperous days.)*—Thus backed by the Englifh nation, it is impoffible they can become bankrupts, and the falfhood of Fox's affertion is of courfe as clear as noon-day.

As to the commutation act it is above all praife. Merchants in general are men of the world, and India merchants certainly rank with the very firft in this excelience. Nothing can be more unmerchantable than crowding a ware-room with an unfaleable commodity, which originally coft fomething, not daring to vend it. Under this mortification ftood the Company, refpecting what they call *bad tea*, and what the public call *good poifon*. This article had been, it feems, thefe twenty years paft in that exact plight, to which its re-afcending muft reduce a great many of the King's liege fubjects—it lay concealed from the fweet face of heaven deep in the cells of the Company's granaries, rending in darknefs, and waiting for a glorious refurrection.

THE power of nations is vulgarly fuppofed to confift in their population, but mifchiefs have often refulted to adminiftrations from *too numerous a body* of fubjects. Wife governments have fometimes undertaken wars for the exprefs purpofe of thinning and tempering their
domi-

dominions, and fome good Kings and minifters have taken means more direct to produce the fame benefit, as in the cafe of .
Chriftian II. and his good Cardinal who difpatched above four hundred refractory fubjects
in one night at a f.aft. That in paffing the
commutation act, Pitt meant to ftrengthen
his miniftry, from that epidemic depopula-
tion of the country, which this tea muft infallibly produce, were an agreeable fpeculation, I confefs, but with all my partiality
for his genius, I cannot fufpect him of fo
profound a motive. Infinite good will undoubtedly refult from the effect of it upon
the health of the people, and all it wants
to be the moft accomplifhed of events is the
certainty of being planned upon *fo* large a
fcale—but I think it was not. Fate that
favoured him in all his other tranfactions,
perhaps imbued this project with a good he
never meant. The higheft ftretches of perfection are hit off by accident, and in this
celebrated meafure the Minifter feems to
have fnatched a bleffing beyond the reach
of defign.

His views were purely confined to the
gratification of the Company. They could
have never fold *this* tea unfhielded by
this act. The duty to the public is taken
off, and the expence to individuals not no-
ticeably diminifhed, for it leaves the price of
their .

their own commodity to their own difcretion*
It is conceived upon this ingenious principle,
that the lefs a man gets for his goods the more
will be his profit upon them. By the *law*,
they are to fell *out*, if one penny be offered
for each lot above the Company's eftimate.
By the *fact* they buy *in*, after confiderable bid-
ding, and then avow their breach of the law.
—And after all, what are the objections to
this act?—mere declamation—only " That
" as a *tax*, it is a grievous oppreffion—
" that as *a commutation* it is an infamous
" fraud—that it is unjuft and cruel, where
" poverty prevents, or where conftitution pro-
" hibits the ufe of the article commuted---
" that it is otherwife an impudent robbery,
" and felling the nation for the fupport of
" thefe rapacious men---that, according to
" Lord Stormont, it is wrenching his
" wretched pittance from the hard hand
" of the poor peafant, merely to fupply
" the prodigality of the India Company,"
(which objection, by the way, Lord Thurlow completely refuted by affirming that the
neceffaries of life, and *not* the luxuries, were
fit objects of taxation) --- " That the act
" (take it all and all) is the moft confum-
" mate piece of infulting knavery ever im-
" pofed upon the people of England."---
That the people of England are the only fuf-
ferers by it, in reality purges it of every
E   crime.

crime. Who is the people of England? An undefined animal capable of bearing, and therefore proper to be preffed with every weight. An afs that brays a little under his burthen, and is then filenced by his own noife, into an infipid tamenefs — goaded by the driver, and fometimes grunting under his pain, but ftill waddling onward fulky and fpiritlefs.

PROFOUND is the wifdom of making a nation *feel* it has a government, and abftracted from this deep policy, the power of the India Company in the Houfe of Commons alone, would juftify the miniftry if they had mortgaged the rentall of the whole kingdom for their fupport. Were this new window tax fifty-fold oppreffive, the public are gainers by commuting it for the fingle acceffion of Major Scott himfelf. A genius who will write a hundred pamphlets in a month, and give them gratis to the public—of fuch exquifite merits too that, except the trouble of reading them, no-body ever charged them with a fault, and that evil is flight, for his own affociates have feldom rifked it, after the firft fample of his literary prowefs.

‘ Sleeplefs himfelf to give his readers fleep.’

THEN have they not the governor, the great Chief himfelf.--“ Have they not *Warren*, is not *Haftings* theirs ?” --- We have heard much of what is called the frontlefs inconfiftency of the prefent adminiftration in their Indian alliances, efpecially againft the incomparable chairman of that fecret Committee, which

which brought the ruin of India home to Haftings. Towards Haftings they affirm, that
Dundas has proved the moft profligate fyco-
phant---towards the Company, the moft un-
principled apoftate that ever defiled the name
of manhood. But, in truth, his conduct to,
both is the tip top of magnanimity, and the
perufal of the forty-fecond refolution, which
he moved in the Houfe of Commons upon
Eaft India concerns, will prove it.

RESOLVED, " That Warren Haftings, Efq.
" Governor General in Bengal, and William
" Hornby, * Efq. Prefident of the Council at
" Bombay, *having, in fundry inftances, acted in*
" *a manner repugnant to the honour and policy of*
" *this nation, and thereby brought great calamities*
" *on India, and enormous expences on the Eaft*
" *India Company, it is the duty of the Directors*
" *of the faid Company, to purfue all legal and ef-*
" *fectual means for the removal of the faid Go-*
" *vernor General and Prefident from their faid*
" *offices, and to recal them to Great Britain."*

AND, alas! who can wonder that the mer-
ciful mind of Dundas fhould be illumined into
a right fenfe of that wonder-working man,
who has brought the very extremes of the
human heart into unifon, and converted the
moft *foft* and the moft *favage* natures in this
ifland to the worfhip of his virtues. When
Thurlow---but what is Thurlow?—What
is the ferocious friendfhip of Thurlow

* Mr. Hornby is in London, for *his* indigence left him power-
lefs in the Court of Proprietors. He is very poor, but then he
is contented.

to the melting devotion of the Queen of
England? The glory of the miniftry is proportioned to the guilt of Haftings, in which
view perhaps fome men will think their fame
incapable of more celebrity. His ufes muft
indeed be great, for his alliance impofed a
weighty tax upon them, and the following
fhort fketch of his atchievements, under their
different heads, is given only to enable the
reader to form a right judgment upon the
fingular merits of that virtuous confederacy.
The recital is taken from the various details
formed out of the records and the authentic
papers of the Eaft India Company, from the
public difpatches of Mr. Haftings himfelf,
and the teftimony of perfons concerned in
the fame tranfactions. Nothing is invented,
and a great deal is fuppreffed.---Whatever
fentence the public may pafs upon the events
ftated, the veracity of the ftatement will not,
I prefume, be denied by any perfon of any
party.

And FIRST of TREATIES.

Treaty with the *Grand Mogul*---for his numberlefs friendfhips to the Company, a folemn fettlement to pay him 260,000*l*. a
year.---Never paid him a fhilling!
Second Treaty with the *Mogul*---agreed to
pay the Soubah of Bengal 400,000*l*.------
Broke this likewife.
Third Treaty with the *Mogul*---agreed to pay
Nudjif Cawn a penfion for fignal fervices

ac-

acknowledged—Broke the treaty and ſtop-
ped the penſion.

Treaty with the *Nizam*—Broken.

Treaty with *Hyder Ally*—Broken.

Treaty with the *Mahrattas*—In profound
peace invaded their country and took Sal-
ſette. Peace made and a treaty eſtabliſhed.
—The treaty broke ſoon after, and the
Mahrattas dominions invaded a ſecond
time. The Company's army defeated.
Moderate terms offered by the Mahrattas,
rejected by *Haſtings*, and vigorous efforts
made to carry on the war, when Hyder
Ally ruſhed into the Carnatic under a confederacy formed by the moſt diſcordant
powers in India for the purpoſe of driving
the Engliſh out of it, as enemies of the
human ſpecies !

Various Treaties with *Mahratta Chiefs*---made
for the ſake of being broken. The obſervance of any two of them would have
brought two Britiſh armies to cut each
others throats.

Treaty with *Ragonaut Row*---that he ſhould
be raiſed to the throne of the Mahrattas,
and placed out of the reach of danger
from the people, (who mortally hated him)
if he aſſiſted in the war.---He aſſiſted in
the war, acquired no throne, and was ſur-
rendered up to the people who mortally
hated him.

Treaty

Treaty with the *Guickwar*---that he should
have a share of the conquests, and be free
from the dominion of the Mahrattas if he
assisted in the war.—He assisted in the war,
got not a foot of the conquests, and was placed
under the dominion of the Mahrattas.

Treaty with the *Rana* of *Gohud*---that he
should have eleven sixteenths of our joint
conquests, and a surety of protection, if
he assisted in the war---He assisted in the
war, did not obtain a mole-hill, but he
got a promise of protection in the treaty,
and at the very moment its ratification was
exchanging, his castle was besieged, his
territories laid waste, and his agent pro-
hibited complaining of this perfidy, by
being denied admission to Mr. Hastings.

General Sacrifice of the *Mahratta Chiefs* and
Princes.---After engaging all that he could
of these people in the war against their
own countrymen, they were abandoned
to the fury of their enemies by an article
in the supplemental treaty whereby " the
" Company is bound not to afford refuge
" to any Chief, Merchant, or other person,
" flying from the Mahrattas into their
" dominion !

STATE of our ALLIES in INDIA.

Ragonaut Row, the *Guickwar*, and the *Rana*
of *Gohud*---ruined.

Grand Mogul---in every misery.

Nabob of *Oude*---in want and servitude.

Rajah

Rajah of *Benares*---in banifhment.
Nabob of *Bengal*—in beggary.
Rajah of *Tanjour*—deftroyed, and his people
perifhing under every diftrefs.
The *Polygars*---ftarving or exiled.
Nabob of *Arcott*---under every calamity.

SALES of STATES and PRINCES.

The *Grand Mogul*---fold to Sujah Dowla.
The *Mogul*'s Territories---fold to the fame
Sujah for two years purchafe.
The *whole nation* of the *Rohillas* fold to the
fame Sujah Dowla, for 4co,ooo *l.* Our
army affifted in butchering this people, and
laying wafte the whole country with fire and
fword. The wife and children of their
Chief, the moft valiant and accomplifhed
man in India, whofe head was cut off and
fold for a fixed fum, were reduced to the ne-
ceffity of begging rice in the Englifh
camp to fupport human nature. The
Englifh commander in this expedition
expreffed fome horror at fuch diabolical
brutalities as he foolifhly deemed them.
He was very properly reprimanded by the
Governor for his officious humanity.*
Serega Dowla—fold to Mir Jaffier.
Mir Jaffier---in his turn to Mir Coffim.
Mir Coffim---back to Mir Jaffier.
Mir Jaffier again---to his eldeft fon.

---

* Major Scott's juftification of this war is moft conclufive,
for, fays the Major " Sir Robert Barker declared the Rohillas
" were a very treacherous people."

Maborec

Maburec ull Dowlah---to his own ſtep-mother,

The *Mahrattas*---ſold to Ragobah.

Ragobah---ſold to the Mahrattas.

The *Mahrattas* an*a Ra_obah*---both offered for ſale to the Rajah of Berar.

Scindia of *Malva*---offered to the ſame.

The *Subah* of the *Decan*---ſold to the Nabob of Arcott.

Hyder Ally---to ditto.

Rajah of *Tanjore*---to ditto.

Twelve Sovereign Princes---to ditto. The Nabob of Arcott was the beſt of all theſe cuſtomers---but even he in his turn was ſold to his own ſon *Amir ul Omrah*.

CONDITION of PLACES *directly* under our DOMINION.

The whole *Kingdom* of *Bengal* was put up to the beſt bidder (as a good means of re‑lieving the country after a famine) and all the Princes, nobility, gentry, free‑holders, farmers, manufacturers, eſtabliſh‑ments, lands, tenements and hereditaments, *ſold*. (It is remarkable that after this auction the Banyan of Mr. Haſtings poſſeſſed territories that yielded him a rent of 140,000 *l.* ſterling a year). Such is the ex‑cellent diſcipline of this Governor General, that perſons who had formerly paid a quit-rent of 200,000 *l.* a year to the Company, now exiſt upon common cha‑rity.

The

The *Carnatic*---ravaged and deftroyed.
Tanjour---in univerfal defolation and decay.

CONDITION of PLACES *indirectly*
under our DOMINION.

Oude—once paid to the government three
millions fterling annually—not one million three hundred thoufand at prefent.
This whole kingdom was confifcated.

Benares—The Rajah of this province paid
his annual tribute 260,000 *l.* as fpe-
cified in his treaty with the Company.
Haftings broke the treaty, and made
a new demand upon him (five lacks
of rupees.) The Rajah pleaded the
treaty, and Haftings accufed him of rebellion. An army was marched againft
the Rajah, and he was forced to pay the
exaction twice. The exaction was demanded a third time, and the Rajah failed to pay it from pofitive want. Haftings fined him in 500,000 *l.* for the failure,
(over and above the tribute and the exaction)
afterwards feized him in his palace, difgraced him in the eyes of his fubjects,
banifhed him his own kingdom, and
placed another upon his throne *.

Fitzula

* Major Scott defends this meafure with great ability and
effect; for, fays the major, " Cheyt Singe was not a fovereign
" prince, he was *only a Zemindar.*" In the fame forcible ftile
he

Fitzula Cawn—paid his tribute of 150,000*l.*
a year to the Company, according to
treaty. Haftings demands 300,000*l.* a
year additional. Fitzula pleaded the treaty,
and Haftings accufed him of rebellion.
Forced to pay 150,000 *l. (over and above
the flipulated tribute)* as a teft of his loyalty.

It was reported that the father of the Rajah of Benares, left his fon a million private-
ly; when Haftings heard the report, he accufed the Rajah of rebellion. —After the ex-
pulfion of this Rajah, it was reported that
his mother *Panna* had great treafures. *Panna* was accufed, and her caftle befieged. She
capitulated upon terms of fafety to her
own perfon and her woman, and the capitulation was folemnly ratified. Yet the *Pauna*
and three hundred women who attended her,
were defpoiled in the night time of all they
poffeffed. The treafures of the caftle, exclufive of the robbery, exceeded 200,000*l.*
and Haftings quarrelled with the Captors concerning the booty.—The mother and grand-
mother of the Nabob of Oude, were reported
to be very wealthy. Haftings accufed them

---

he defends the maffacre of the Rohillas, for, fays the Major,
" the progenitors of the Rohillas were not natives, they
" were a race of Afghan Tartars," and for the proof of this,
refers you to Dow's Hiftory of Hindoftan. The *Englifh* in
India vindicate the extirpation of an entire people, and the ruin
of a prince, becaufe the anceftors of the people were not natives, and the prince was not an hereditary fovereign!

of

of rebellion, and they were obliged twice to
affert their allegiance by the furrender of
their treafures. Their powers of rebellion
confifted in an army of two thoufand women, and two feraglios of eunuchs.

(ALTHOUGH in the eyes of fome fcrupulous puritanical people, Mr. Haftings may
appear fomewhat erroneous now and then,
his capacity is unqueftionable, and the miniftry in their patronage of him, without
doubt, mean to blefs us with his abilities in
fome public office at home. His plan of finance
would be a fertile fource of fuccour in this
kingdom, as it is in India. Charges of treafon
now and then againft the Bedfords, the Devon-
fhires, the Fitzwilliams, the Marlboroughs,
the Norfolks, and other poffeffors of great
fortunes in enmity to the King's friends, would
be an infinite mine of revenue. Between Haftings's rebellions, and Pitt's commutations, the
national debt muft infallibly be redeemed in
a fhort time.)

VIOLATION of ORDERS.

The DIRECTORS.	HASTINGS.
We do not approve the treaty of Poor-under, but ftill we are d. termined to ad-here to it ftrictly.	*Broke this treaty immediately.*

We command you at all events not to involve us in war.

Commenced the Mahratta war directly.

We think Mr. Francis Fowke a very fit perfon to be refident at Benares.

Recalled him from his refidence at Benares and faid the Company invaded " his prerogative."

We pofitively defire that you will reftore Mr. Fowke to his ftation.

Your Empire fhould fink into the ocean firft.

In our opinion Mr. John Briftow is a fit perfon to be refident at Lucknow.

Recalled him from Lucknow directly.

Upon confideration we acquiefce in the recall of Mr. Briftow from Lucknow.

Nay then, he fhall go back to Lucknow ; and back he fent him.

We are of opinion that you have treated Cheyt Singe with cruelty, injuftice, and impolicy, and ftrictly charge you to reftore him to his throne and kingdom.

If he comes within my reach I'll ftrangle the rafcal.

We defire that you will advertife all contracts, that you will give preference to the loweft bidder, and that

Advertifes no contract ; rejects the loweft offers, gives preference to his own friends, and fixes the duration of

each contract shall be of only one year's duration.

When the present Nabob of Bengal succeeded his father, he was a minor. The Directors thus order their servant : " We desire that you " will appoint a Mi- " nister to transact " the affairs of the " government, and to " select for that pur- " pose some person " well qualified for " the affairs of govern- " ment, to be Minister " of the government, " and guardian of the " Nabob's minority."

each, at five years in- stead of one.

Appointed Munny Begum, *a woman who had formerly belonged to a company of dancing girls, and whom the late Nabob took a liking to, and after some coha- bitation married. By the Eastern customs, this woman was shut up in the seraglio from the eyes and the intercourse of society—yet she was solemnly invested with all the functions of go- vernment, and made guardian of the young Nabob. His own mo-* ther *was then alive in the seraglio, but Hast- ings chose his* step-mo- ther " *as a person well* " *qualified for the af-* " *fairs of government* " *for the office of a Mi-* " *nister, and for the guar-* " *dianship of a Prince.*"*

MONEY.

* A minute of General Clavering, Colonel Monson, and Mr. Francis upon this business, concludes in these words— " *It*

M O N E Y.

BEFORE we examine the clandeſtine receipt of money, it is right to obſerve the
terms of the Act of Parliament upon that
ſubject. Theſe are the words. " That no
" *Governor General*, or any of the council,
" ſhall directly, or indirectly, accept, re-
" ceive, or take, of or from any perſon, or
" perſons, or *on any account whatſoever*, any
" preſent, gift, donation, gratuity, or re-
" ward, pecuniary or otherwiſe."—Now
for the obſervance of the act.

Firſt Sum—*Twenty-three thouſand pounds from*
Cheit Singe.

Second Sum—*Thirty-four thouſand five hun-*
dred pounds. From whom this preſent
came never appeared.

Third Sum—*Sixteen thouſand pounds.* The
donor unknown.

Fourth Sum—*Twenty-three thouſand eight hun-*
dred and ſeventy-one pounds. The donor unknown.

The firſt ſum Mr. Haſtings *ſaid* he paid
into the hands of the ſub-treaſurers at Cal-
cutta—but the Company never received *any*
other account that it really was paid—For

" *We believe there never was an inſtance in India of a truſt ſo*
" *diſpoſed of!*" In page 81, the reader will find ſomething
which perhaps he may deem explanatory of this appoint-
ment.

the

the fecond fum he takes bonds of the Company, as if the money was his own, and afterwards relinquifhes a part of it as the Company's right. It is all his own at one time, only two thirds of it at another, and at laft he furrenders his whole claim of it.--- For the third fum he likewife takes a bond as if the money was all his own, and in fome time after he yields the entire back again to the Company.---The fourth fum he likewife claimed as his own at one time, and abandoned at another time as the Company's property.

There is befide thefe a claim made by Mr. Haftings upon the Company of *twenty-nine thoufand pounds* for Durbar charges. In fome time after however, he recollects that *this* money alfo belonged to the Company, and remits the claim---*(The reader fhould be informed, that Mr. Haftings never acknowledged the receipt of any monies thus acquired, until after Mr. Francis took his paffage for England, and after the Houfe of Commons had appointed the two Committees to enquire into the Company's affairs.)* Fifth Sum---*One hundred thoufand pounds*, a prefent to Mr. Haftings by the Subah of Oude. (The Subah owed the Company an enormous debt at the fame time.)

THIS fum was paid by bills on a great money lender of Benares, and the negociation of the bills rendered the concealment of
the

the tranfaction next to impoffible. Mr.
Haftings took a particular fancy to this prefent, and begged the Company would let
him have it. The Company refufed his re-
queft, and referred him to the Act of Parliament. The Act declares all prefents to
be the property of the Company, but not as
a fanction for receiving them, which the
Act pofitively prohibits. The view is only
" to inveft the Company with a legal title to
" a civil fuit." *By his own confeffion Mr.*
Haftings received 228,000 l. *in about one year
and five months of this forbidden money.*

MISCELLANEOUS CHARGES.

Tippo Saib---The Mahrattas in the treaty in-
fifted an article fhould be inferted to give
Hyder, or his fon (Hyder foon after died)
the benefit of peace, if he chofe to accept it,
and Haftings ordered Anderfon to admit
in the treaty a claufe to that fenfe. But
here he difplayed infinite faculty---for *at
the very moment* he admitted an article to
make peace with Tippo Saib, he projected
a plan with Madagee Scindia for his
*total deftruction, and actually parcelled out his
dominions to be divided between them.* .

I am aware that fome puny infirm mortals will be apt to exclaim a little upon
this occafion (the cruelties our prifoners received under Tippoo being
frefh in their memory) and perhaps the
juftice of Providence will be queftioned---
Why

Why does the poor foldier or fubaltern guiltlefs of this infamous treachery *fuffer*, and they who wantonly provoked this bar-barity, lord it in all the banefulnefs of, triumphant impunity ? The goodnefs of Providence too perhaps may be implored, to give fome confolation to the thoufands that lament at this moment in the bitternefs of anguifh, the hard fate of their dear relatives who fell the victims of a fevere though juft retaliation.—But after all, there would be more piety than pclicy in fuch exclamations ! We know that battles were never fo defperately fought, as when the wife cuftom prevailed of cutting off the prifoners heads after dinner ; and the revival of that ufeful valour which fprings from the certainty of death to captives, was, I doubt not, one of Mr. Haftings's motives in ftimulating Tippo Saib to this exemplary rigour.

Munny Begum---Receiving *one million fifty thoufand rupees* from Munny (the Nabob's *Minifter* and *Guardian*) for AN ENTERTAINMENT --- This he never denied, but reproached his colleagues* bitterly

---

* GENERAL Clavering, Colonel Monfon, and Mr. Francis. Thefe Gentlemen make the following declaration in a minute, dated May 25, 1775.—" In the late proceedings of " the Revenue Board it appears that there is *no fpecies of pe-* " *culation* from which the *Governcr General* has thought prc- " per to abftain."

F   for

for making the difcovery. It certainly was very impolite.

Phoufedar of *Hughly*---Difpoffeffing a man of this office, and appointing another in his place, with a falary of 72,000 rupees per annum, out of which falary Haftings himfelf was to have 36,000, and his Banyan, for managing the bufinefs, 4000 more.

THE reader will find this curious affair at large in the eleventh report of the felect Committee, with its appendix, and it is really worth his perufal. Haftings difcovered infinite ability in the evafion of enquiries into thefe and many other charges. To ufe the words of the poet ' No man has a more " engaging prefence of mind on the road." His genius fparkles with greater refulgence in proportion to the magnitude of his danger. We underftand the gaining over, or buying off an enemy, indifferently well in this country—promotion, bribery, retirement, and many other dextrous devices are familiar to us. But the beft among us are botches in the art. Set our boldeft efforts befide Haftings, and what a contemptible figure they make! A grievous charge lay againft him at a particular time, and in the whole world there was but one * man who could injure him---It was no feafon for indecifion, and his expedient was at leaft equal to

* Nundcomar.

the

the peril. He indicted the man for a conspiracy, and failing in that, he accufed him of a new crime, and the man was *hanged* directly. The moft captivating theory in Machiavel is mere milkinefs to this method of filencing an enemy. In that hour and in that act, perifhed *all* the accufers of Mr. Haftings in the *Eaft.*

THE fame fplendid capacity is difplayed upon every exigency. His judgment told him once, it would be right to refign his office, and he difpatched an agent (Mr. Maclean) for this exprefs purpofe. The refignation was formally notified and formally accepted. His judgment afterwards told him it would be wrong to refign, and then he folemnly denied having confided any fuch commiffion to the agent whom he difpatched for that very purpofe. Should he---who yefterday could fay unto his kneeling flave, " Rife up and be a king"---become the willing inftrument of his own degradation !--- fhould he, who funk the defcendant of Tamerlane into fhame and want, fink himfelf into a private citizen of this country !--- fhould that ftar that luminates a world, twinkle through the ftreets of this faucy town unnoticed perhaps, or noticed only to be defpifed! and furrender the gorgeous grandeur of his prefent fituation on the defperate rifk of fading into the falfe glare and counterfeit honor of a Britifh Peerage !

NEVER

NEVER was man ftored with truer notions of good government than this great man. A cobler in Fetter-lane defies all the powers of the King of England to deprive him of an old ftrap more than the law allows him.---But fee how it fares with the owner of a kingdom under Mr. Haftings. " The Company, " or the perfon delegated by the Company " holds an abfolute authority over the fub- " ject (the owner of a kingdom), that fub- " ject owes an *implicit* and *unreferved* obedi- " ence to this authority, at the forfeiture " even of his *life* and *property* at the *difcretion* " of thofe who hold or fully reprefent the fo- " vereign authority, and that authority is " fully delegated to *me!*"—Thefe are the words of Mr. Haftings, and every body knows he is not a man of *words,* (except indeed to the Company.) Unlike fome pigeon-livered poffeffors of uncontrouled fway in Europe, who are coldly content with having it, *he* fcorns an inert authority, and cannot be arraigned for having left any power he ever acquired by any means, unexerted in a fingle inftance.

THE fame fuperior character beams through his policy with foreign ftates. " I fhall be " always ready to profefs," fays this great man in a blaze of fpirit and franknefs,— " that one of *my* motives for going to war " with *my neighbours,* is the hope of getting " their *wealth.*" — And the moral of this fhining

fhining fentiment is the type of his life, for
no man was born of woman whofe principles and practice harmonize in truer unifon.

HE has fent a peace-offering in his
laft letter, for his vifit to *Lucknow* procured from the Nabob 450,000*l.*—How
procured he beft knows! but his merit
muft be infinite, when the misfortunes
of that country, from the inflictions of
God, are added to its miferies from
this *demi-god*. His letter contains mani-
fold confolations to this nation—he tells us
that our empire in India (an empire eftablifhed above a hundred years) exifts only
upon the " *thread of opinion.*"---and to
crown our comfort, this thread is held by
Warren Haflings !

His letter has been publifhed on the very
day* I am writing this paffage ; and without the fmalleft apprehenfion of being con-
tradicted, I affirm, that it is the moft
curious and entertaining epifttle that ever
attracted the notice of mankind, from the
time of Scaurus and Beftia, to the time of
Haftings.

OVERLOOKING (if that were poffible) the
high wrought touches of this unequalled
piece of writing, and not adverting to
dates or fignatures, you would imagine, not
only that Haftings and the Company had
changed characters, but that the fituation of
the Earth was altered, and that *they* were to
execute, *he* to *advife* : for the whole letter is

* The 17th of January,

F 3   made

made up of cenfures and of precepts; of their
ignorance and roguery by implication, his
own abilities and integrity in direct terms.

As for its ftile, no criticifm can reach it.
Indeed it is a compendium of ftiles, and
every line of it, like the text of the great
clafficks, would bear a folio of commentaries.

As an inftance of the *fublime*—the Prince
of Delhi comes to Lucknow. " *An uncom-*
" *mon phenomenon has fuddenly appeared, which*
" *though in itfelf fimple and unimportant, has de-*
" *rived a magnitude, like the lefs ordinary events*
" *of the phyfical world, viewed through the me-*
" *dium of fuperftition, from its operation on the*
" *opinions of mankind.*"

OF the *eafy*—he changes his lodgings.
" *On the fame obvious motives, the Prince having*
" *defired to be accommodated in a houfe near to*
" *my own, I refigned to him that which I then*
" *occupied, and took immediate poffeffion of one of*
" *the Nabob's, which he had originally provided*
" *and prepared for my reception, within the com-*
" *pafs of his own palace, and immediately adjoin-*
" *ing to that which he lives in.*"

INCORRUPTION.—" *Few are the advocates of*
" *the national interefts, and their voice will be*
" *faintly heard amid the numerous and loud ex-*
" *clamations of private rapacity; but I humbly*
" *affume to rank myfelf with* THE FORMER."

MODERATION.—" *God forbid that any future*
" *Pizarro's and Almagro's fhould difgrace the*
" *annals of your dominion, or mark the traces of*
" *its decline with the blood, &c.*"

THE mad, or the true no meaning. " *That*
" *fource*

" *source, which ought to flow with the princi-*
" *ples of its duration, will, if productive of the*
" *same deleterious streams, which have been late-*
" *ly seen to issue from it, prove the cause of its*
" *diffolution.*"

PERHAPS it is on purpose to be misunder-
stood, that all his letters are full of these non-
intelligibles. But let us deliver up this poe-
tical compoſer of diſpatches, this Pindarick
proſe writer, to the diſpoſal of the critics,
and view him for a moment, as a politician.
After ſtating that no common obſtruction
ſhall reſtrain him from remaining in his ſitu-
ation, until he brings certain good projects
of his own to perfection, he ſays, " I poſſeſs
" ſuch inherent advantages, as I truſt will
" prove ſuperior to every ſpecies of oppoſi-
" tion, but the laſt extremity of it."—In ſo
many words, I will not ſtir one inch, for
all your authorities—when he wrote this
letter he had heard that Mr. Fox's bill had
been read twice in the Houſe of Commons,
but knew nothing of the change of miniſtry, and concluding that he would be recalled by the late adminiſtration, he thus
prepares the nation for a determined reſiſt-
ance. He is well inſtructed as to the popular clamours in London, as this paſſage will
ſhew. " It was the condition of vaſſalage
" and meanneſs to which the ſervants of the
" king of Delhi had reduced him, by de-
" grading him into a mere inſtrument of
" their intereſted and ſordid deſigns, that he
" regretted. _

THE

THE attachment of the princes and chiefs muft fpring from pofitive infpiration. Except the grand Mogul, whom he has ftarved, the Vizier " whom he has cut to the bones?" the Rajah of Benares, whom he has banifhed, and Nundcomar, whom he has hanged, no two *men* in India (women indeed have) fuffered more from this glorious governor, than Fitzula, and Almafs Ally Cawn. The former however is now fo reconciled, that he fent his fon to Lucknow to confirm the affurance of his attachment to the *Company* and the *Britifh nation*; and Almafs Ally, the miferable victim of the moft inhuman perfecution, is now it feems, eager and anxious to teftify his love for this mercilefs author of all his calamities. The Prince of Delhi's vifit is, without doubt, purely *accidental*, and Haftings in fending him to Madagee Scindia, takes indeed the moft effectual of all methods, " to preferve the tranquility of our poffeffions."---Now lives there a man who would imagine that the author of thefe heavy oppreffions upon the unfortunate Mogul, upon the Vizier, Almafs Ally Cawn, and the different other perfons whofe caufe he pleads in this letter with the moft fpecious humanity was the very perfon himfelf who fo defcribes them ?—and in India, or in Europe, or in the whole world, is there fuch another inexplicable being as this Governor General of Bengal ?

Such is the letter and the letter writer. With all his merits he had been a dead weight

weight upon the miniftry, if they had not fortunately influenced the moft facred perfonage in this country, by her reception of his wife, and by the fanction of her fmiles, to give operation to his powers, and currency to his character.

NOTHING lefs could ferve the great end in view. Not the burthen of ten thoufand hawkers freighted daily by the unfatigued eternal Major.---Nor the recantation of Dundas, nor all his flimy panegyrics---nor the perfpicuous inanities of Pitt---nor the barbarous growling of Thurlow, could ftem the torrents that flowed from the Reports of the Committees.---Even *Robinfon Crufoe* * failed. The cordial hug of Mrs. Haftings, frefh in oriental fragrance, and blooming in all her unpolluted virtues, could alone turn their Indian fyftem in favour of the prefent, and throw a ftigma upon the late miniftry---thofe bad men who had fo bafely perfecuted the moft fpotlefs hufband of the moft fpotlefs wife in Chriftendom.

ONE of the chief aims (and I think one of the beft aims) of the King's friends, is the levelling of all moral diftinctions, and equalizing the characters of mankind, without any diftinction whatever---infomuch that the prefervation of an exact balance, betwixt their own, and even the royal reputation, has been ftudioufly and uniformly fought by

* LORD Thurlow faid, the Reports of the Houfe of Commons had juft as much weight with him, as reading Robinfon Crufoe.

them.

them. Nothing is more invidious among
the great, than an infulting fuperiority
in the virtues, and a moft generous fel-
lowfhip has been dealt (with a moft equi-
table reciprocity in the fpirit of this principle) between the mafter and fervants, fo
that neither party ever feels the leaft concern for any thing that might injure the
fame of the other party. There are, who
impute to the operation of this good maxim, the perfuafions of the Miniftry in favour of Mrs. Haftings.---Whatever the motive was, they have certainly fucceeded ; and
the Queen's mortification, upon a conceffion
unprecedented in her hiftory, cannot be efti-
mated on a better fcale, than by the reflection
of her own connubial character, and the determined diftance at which fhe has fyfte-
matically kept every woman however fplendid her rank, or powerful her influence, on
whom fufpicion had laid her fingers---*before
this inftance.*

In *my* judgment the Miniftry were impelled by wifer and worthier incitements, than
injuring the character or feelings of the facred perfon alluded to. To purge the country
of a national ftain, and produce in the fame act,
a national benefit, were I doubt not their
objects. Philofophers admit that virtues
in the extreme do operate as vices. The
Britifh Court has long been reproached for
an unpolifhed diftafte of certain female ele-
gancies, that gamefomnefs of moral, and that
agreeable loofenefs of principle which bring
about

about occafional deviations from the inhuman
and barbarous reftraints of the marriage bond,
and which contribute greatly to the perfection
of the female mind. Many good people have
juftly decried this fqueamifhnefs, and it certainly has furnifhed foreign nations with inftruments of flander againft us, as a fet of
iflanders, a parcel of favages, blind to the true
delights and luxuries of life.---We all know
the marked difcouragement which the firft
female in the land has uniformly fhewn to
every attempt at reforming this defect, and
it was a moft judicious meafure in the miniftry, now that her royal daughters are gradually growing into womanhood, to attempt the
removal of every poffible impediment to the
formation of thofe foreign alliances which
we have a right to hope through fuch an
amiable medium : by their having introduced
a perfon to be the grace of the royal circle,
the ornament of the Court, whofe character
may tend to wipe away this ftain in the face
of Europe, whofe accomplifhments might
meliorate this rigorous and ruftic virtue, and
from whofe fociety and example the royal
offspring might chance to pick up fome im-
provements that would tend to ftrengthen
their titles to ufeful and fplendid connections
among the princes of Europe. Cardinal
Mazarine removed . the Pyrrhenees and
founded the grandeur of the French monarchy upon the bafis of a royal match. Our
Mazarines have the moft numerous train of
lovely, and hitherto unfullied females, that
                                    ever

ever animated minifters to negociate, and it were indeed lamentable that any coarfe difqualification, like the very furmountable one alluded to, fhould deprefs their efforts for encreafing the glory of the Houfe of Brunfwick ; and adding to the ftrength and fafety of the Britifh empire, in their difpofal of fo divine a progeny.

So much for the fervices of the India Company to the King's friends, and their grateful facrifices in return.

THE PRINCIPLES of a Government are greatly definable from the means ufed to obtain its patronage, and feveral events have occurred within a few months, to elucidate the aims of the prefent miniftry by this rule, as well as to eftablifh in our hearts a confidence in their fincerity.

AGAINST the equal fpirit of the common law of England, and the wicked caution of ftatutes in favour of the fubjects liberty, the friends of the Crown had, upon exigencies, one certain fource of fupport---I mean the twelve Judges, and thofe to do them juftice have feldom failed them. The integrity of Judges has been much blazoned fince the King has been robbed of the power of removing them, but in this affumption there is in reality lefs truth than affectation. The Judges upon being fixed for life, grew rather prudifh than chafte, and had more coquetry than folid paffion in their boafted independence. When the Crown has tried them, the
fame

fame convenient pliancy—the fame temper of expedient ductility, the fame relaxablenefs of mind that characterifed their predeceffors have feldom been wanting (bating fome flight exceptions.) There are indeed fome fierce indomitable fpirits, even now upon the bench, whofe rugged and clumfy attachment to their duties, would, I fear, be proof to the arts of the mighty necromancer, Pitt himfelf—but thefe I truft are not the larger number. Others there are who, on the folemn tribunal of difpenfing the law—in the facred feat of juftice, can yield to their ambitions, and direct the incenfe to the proper channel. The right of juries is one of the worft evils of this conftitution, and the only candidate for the only great judicial office likely to be foon vacated, timed his efforts to abridge thofe pernicious rights moft excellently, and in charging twelve men to convict a fellow fubject, (ftrictly prohibiting the confideration of his guilt) had views far fuperior to the luft of punifhing, or a fanguinary fpirit of perfecution, (though both are undoubtedly laudable paffions in a Judge.) In Sir Francis Buller's charge to the Jury who tried the Dean of St. Afaph, nothing implacable, nothing rancourous to the Dean difgraced his lips. He could owe *him* no perfonal fpite, as he truly obferved, when the judgment was arrefted. He was,

I doubt

I doubt not, utterly indifferent to the point, if the principle was not impaired. Animated with nobler incitements, the learned Judge, confcious that the jury's right of finding general verdicts was one of the beams that fuftain this crazy conftitution, and the very inftrument that produced the odious Revolution, was only anxious to lend his mite to our emancipation, perfuaded that in clipping this darling priviledge of Englifhmen, he was taking the fureft road to the fucceffion of the firft feat of criminal juftice in Great Britain.

INNUMERABLE are the qualifications of this good man for that high office. Some fay he is proud, unfeeling, arbitrary, and cruel. I think he is not, but yet I am fure that all thefe are ingredients requifite for a Judge in thefe times. A miftake on the Bloody fide of the queftion is always fafeft. Criminals are not hanged for the fake of fending the particular wretch out of this world, but for the benefit of example to the public. The more examples therefore, the more benefit, and the murder of innocence is amply attoned in the fervice rendered the community by the execution of a fellow creature.

" *A popular judge is a deformed thing!*" faid a great man. This is a golden fentiment to the King's friends. No popular judge ever anfwered the ends of government,

and

and fuch are the fatal errors of our civil
fyftem, that every judge has been odious to
the people in proportion to his fervility to
the crown. But this dictum juftly fuppofes
them to be fuch a herd of vile abandoned
beings, that a Judge who becomes their favourite muft of neceffity be deformed. It
pulls down that unfortunate barrier between
honor and infamy, the love of fame ; fhelters
a Judge in all that wife and virtuous complaifance to the reigning Minifter which the
conftitutional fanatics term bafenefs, turpitude, and treachery ; for if after felling himfelf, his country, and his office (events
fometimes requifite to government, and perfectly right in the Judge) the national hatred
fhould fall down upon him, he is fteeled in
the coat of mail of this maxim, which, like
the Pope's difpenfation, abfolves him from
every fin.

" A POPULAR Judge is a deformed thing,"
and *fuch a thing* is not Judge Buller. His
whole life has ftudioufly avoided this deformity, and I defy all his enemies to fhew
one inftance of his tranfgreffing againft the
rule. A learned lawyer, and after him a
noble and illuftrious Judge, both quoted
this faying in Juftice Buller's vindication laft
November. I am not jealous of that application : my object in mentioning it is only
to rectify a miftake into which the learned
lawyer and even the noble Judge led the
                                        public

public refpecting the *fource* of this precious
faying. Both attributed it to Judge Fofter.
Now I beg leave, in honour of the fpotlefs
man who was the true author of it, and to
whom the fentiment was more congenial, to
tell the reader that this ineftimable maxim
was *not* Judge Fofter's—It was the maxim of
him, whom a poet dear to that venerable
Judge and to this nation called
‘ The wifeft, brighteft—*meaneft* of mankind.’
—It was the maxim of *Lord Bacon*—a model whom I cordially recommend to Judge
Buller, not from any fympathy that fubfifts
between them in the grofs view of money,
but becaufe a faithful purfuit of his lordfhip's
fteps will lead himfelf to all the dignities of
his profeffion, and greatly accelerate that
happinefs to us which had long fince been
our lot, if men and judges like Judge Fofter
had not officioufly impeded the current of
our good fortune, in oppofition to the Bacon's
and the Buller's of other ages.

VARIOUS circumftances advantageous to
the miniftry occurred upon this trial. The
Judge and the Crown Advocate played the
fame game. The Barrifter would fit on the
bench, and the Judge in the corner would
prefer the center. Mr. Bearcroft in defcanting
upon the wickednefs of telling plain truth
volunteered in the Minifter's caufe, and gave
the *reform* an unbought blow, by ftigma-
tizing the Irifh for their zeal in favour of it.

---In

In his digreffive taunt upon the Irifh Mr.
Bearcroft effentially ferved the Miniftry.
The reproach he caft has been vehemently
reprobated in Ireland, and will tend in its
degree to promote the difcontentednefs of
that country, the increafe of which feems
the great policy of government at this time.
---The Judge taunted the argument for the
rights of Juries ' *as the language of a party*,'
meaning thofe ragamuffins the Whigs, one of
whom defended the Dean as council, and impudently dared in open court to vindicate not
merely the libel (which at fuch a time as
this feditioufly revived the moft pernicious
doctrines in magna charta and the bill of
rights) but likewife the obnoxious right of
Juries to find general verdicts (when it is our
evident intereft to demolifh Juries altogether) as well as the people's right to reform
the Houfe of Commons (when the very name
of a Houfe of Commons fhould be blotted
from our memory)---Such is the virulent
bigotry of that faction in all that regards
this diabolical conftitution !

HERE I muft tell the reader with a tremb-
ling heart my apprehenfions, that the fiend
Fox intends to bring a bill into Parliament this winter, to eftablifh the right of
Juries to find general verdicts, and what
is worfe, I fear that our amiable Minifter
cannot hazard an oppofition to it in the
LowerHoufe, from the peculiar temper of the
G   pre-

prefent moment. This meafure (if the mutes
fhould not ftrangle it above ftairs) would make
againſt us without doubt. But the mifchief
is momentary, for every thing muſt fall by
and by in the common cruſh of the whole
fyſtem. That's our comfort.

THIS conceſſion however is but merely
difcretionary—the Miniſter's power in the
Lower Houfe is in reality omnipotent. Not
Cæfar was more fuccefsful when he raifed
the Centurions into that Senate which courted
flavery, and wifely depoſited all the authorities of the Roman conſtitution in the perfon of an individual, than William Pitt in
modelling the prefent Houfe of Commons.
Scores of legiflators he has made, who expected to fit upon the Britiſh throne, juſt as
much as in the Britiſh parliament, twelve
months ago—Aye, but are they daſhers?—
Is there no dread of conſtituents—no fear of
fhame upon the long run?—Can he truſt
them in *all* cafes?—This I cannot anfwer
for---but he can make Peers of all the doubt-
ful members, and then their faith is infallible while he is miniſter.

THE mention of the peerage fuggeſts an-
other ftrong ground of confidence in the prefent miniſtry. Creating Nobles is a prodigious fource of fupport to the King's friends.
In moſt countries of Europe this prerogative
has been exercifed upon men either of dif-
tinguiſhed family, extenfive properties ho-
nourably

nourably acquired, or eminent profeffional merit---but limited to fuch reftrictions with us, it had been in fact rather an incumbrance than an inftrument of power---*non tali auxilio nec defenforibus iftis tempus eget.* Men of this defcription had never elevated the Britifh Houfe of Lords to the dignity of a Divan, for how could the King's friends depend upon fuch men ?---To fteer wide of this evil, the new miniftry have judicioufly gone to the very oppofite extreme, and overturned the ordinary fyftem fo excellently, that in the conferring of titles the rate of private infult and public indecorum has been the only meafure---A fixed ratio of rank is eftablifhed—the degree proportioned to the ftrength of the alliance. So many votes make an Earl, fo many a Vifcount, &c. Englifh or Irifh---according to the cafe. Mr. Beckford is on the lift for Englifh nobility. By the ratio he has a right to it from his forces in the Lower Houfe.---But I doubted his fuccefs. The fon of *him* (or of his wife,) who dared to fay, that the libellers of his loyal fubjects, were unworthy a King's confidence, had a thin claim upon George the Third—that he was brother to one of the moft implacable remorfelefs Whigs * in Eng-

---

* RICHARD BECKFORD, the prefent member for Arundel (to whom perhaps fome apology is due for putting his name in this page.) Mr. Beckford with his characteriftic pleafantry fays, that he was chofen for Bridport in the year 1780 *becaufe he was a Whig,* and turned out in 1784 *for the fame reafon.*

land,

land, did not furely in fo far augment his
intereft with William Pitt---But *now* his title is unqueftionable.

A SINGLE Stentor—(unlefs difqualified by
any lurking love of independence, or fuf-
pected of latent leanings towards conftitutional doctrines) is entitled by the ratio to
an Englifh baronetage, an Irifh peerage.
more or lefs, *pro re nata.* A vote the lefs
would hardly keep Lord Delaval, for inftance, on the bafe lift of *Irifh* nobility,
gnawing his liver to promote *the caufe* in the
armour of a *Britifh baron.* In apoftacies marked with features of fingular infamy—where
the treachery is frontlefs, and the bafenefs be
of an implicit kind, there are always favorable
difcriminations. Lord North was Delaval's
God fix months ago.

" But merit will by turns forfake them all,
" Would you know when, *exactly when*
    they fall."

It is not the office but the officer that is
divine, and a mifunderftanding of thefe de-
votions was the rock Lord North fplit upon.
He lifted men from the gutter into rank,
and raifed beggars into bankers—" They
" would die rather than defert him—they
" would be the vileft wretches that ever
" ftained the name of men if they aban-
" doned fo honourable, fo liberal a patron."
And he in the confidence of his nature takes
                                                all

all this for granted, as if profeſſion was any ſurety for good faith, or benefaction for gratitude.

Such is the enobling ſyſtem of the King's friends. The late miniſtry too it ſeems *would* make peers—What! pollute the unſtained threſhold of the Houſe of Lords with their crew—ſouls formed of ſteel, fellows made up of that republicaniſm of mind that grates at the very ſound of ſervitude! Hazard a mutiny under the very roof of the ſeraglio!— " The fool was wiſer I thank you."

THE COMPOSITION of the public cabinet beams the brighteſt proſpects upon this nation—The Gower's and the Thurlow's are ſuperior to ſuſpicion—*Their* whole life is one continued chain of demonſtrations of zeal and ſincerity for *the cauſe*. As little reaſon is there to doubt the other members, if their true characters were underſtood. Lord Cambden might perhaps create ſome qualms from ſuſpicions of Whiggiſm. If Lord Cambden had raſhly oppoſed the miniſtry in trampling upon a Houſe of Commons that dared to defy the power, and inſolently rejected the corruptions of government—If Lord Cambden defended the conſtitution when Lord Temple with his intrepid aſſociates made a bold breach in the very centre of it—If Lord Cambden reprobated the

G 3 doctrine

doctrine of originating money bills in the Upper House, and refisted a motion which imputed a breach of law and conftitution to the Commons of England, *for declaring an opinion concerning the public money* ---If Lord Cambden took this courfe, his guilt cannot be concealed ; but having done the very reverfe of it, I maintain that the imputation of Whiggifm is a libel upon his Lordfhip. But let us not be fcared by a bugbear !—What is the name of a Whig ! If Lord Cambden's title to the found were never fo undifputed, we have this fupreme confolation, that his Lordfhip has vindicated fome of the moft comfortable doctrines that ever brufhed from the eyes of mankind, this film called liberty. *Difcretion* and *ftate neceffity* (thofe valuable doctrines which zealots foolifhly call the law of tyrants) have been carried farther by Lord Cambden, than by any other man in this kingdom. Affuming a power to fufpend law coft James II. his crown, and prevented the happinefs of this nation by producing the revolution. This very principle, *whenever the King thinks it wife to fufpend*, has been vindicated by Lord Cambden in fome of the moft fplendid harangues ever delivered in the Houfe of Peers.*

SITUATION has amazing influence upon fome politicians, and if the Chancellorfhip, in

---

* SEE the debates upon the corn proclamation in 1768.

the

the bloom of his abilities feventeen years fince, perfuaded Lord Cambden into the excellence of this laft and greateft of James the Second's principles, it is a fair prefumption that the Prefidency of the Council at his prefent time of life, impaired in faculties, and ftrengthened by years and by experience in that love of the good things of this world infeparable from old age, and againft which the enmity of lawyers in particular is not very uniform, will impel him to compliances far more liberal and decifive.

But are there not others in the public cabinet challengeable for affection to this *great caufe?* Stands not the Duke of Richmond committed upon points directly adverfe to the demolition of this conftitution?—From all anxiety in this refpect I fhall have little difficulty in refcuing the reader. I do admit that the Duke of Richmond, encumbered with principles in any meafure adequate to his profeffions, might be an impediment: but the big breaftwork of conftitutional defence erected by his Grace in the days of his oppofition to the King's friends, is in truth reduced to the level of his own military genius, and the capture of this conftitution will be juft as effectually obftructed by *his* political fyftem, as the capture of the kingdom by his *fortifications*, if it was invaded by an enemy.

RESISTANCE to infidelity, where there is much temptation to it, is a good teft of faith;

and religious cafuifts have raifed obftacles to the univerfality of their own fyftems, neceffary perhaps to encreafe the merit of believers, but fo crouded with contradictions as rendered them very troublefome to reconcile. Whether any myftical motive of this kind has brought the Duke of Richmond into this prefent predicament, is not eafy to afcertain; but this I affirm, that I would fooner undertake with Erafmus* to prove, that the horfe which he ftole from Sir Thomas More, had been in Flanders and in England at one and the fame moment, than to reconcile the Richmond of eighty-one, with the Richmond of eighty-four. Athenafius himfelf was an Euclid to him. Indeed he is made up of paradoxes.

CONSISTENCY in the new allies would be fatal to our welfare, and all of them who have vindicated their claim to *our* affections by a fincere dereliction of their former principles, and a thorough oblivion of paft declarations, opinions, and doctrines, *fhould* have our affections. Foremoft in this line of fervice ftands his Grace the Duke of Richmond, as the reader will fee from this brief review.

THE Duke faid, he never deferted and never would defert his friends—in eighty-two he kept, and in eighty-three recovered, his place

---

* Quod mihi fcripfifti, de corpore Chrifti,
    Crede quod edes, et *edes*;
  Sic tibi refcribo, de tuo paltrido,
    Crede quod habes, et *habes*.

by

by their down-fall and his defertion. He ever
was, and ever will be a whig—he fupport-
ed every effort of the King's friends for the
laft twelve months, which radically over-
turns the whole fyftem of whiggifm. He
ever was, and will ever be an enemy to coalitions—he is linked in bonds of dearnefs with
Gower and Thurlow, Dundas and Jenkinfon.
He ever was, and ever will be a foe to fecret
influence—he bends every day with a contrite
reverence to the high priefts of the temple.
He always did, and always will, oppofe the
influence of the crown—he lately helped to
encreafe it beyond all former examples. He
had fo little regard for the perfon of his fovereign, that he refufed a mark of decorum
fhewn in all civilized nations to the reigning
prince, and publicly* proclaimed his contempt
for it—he is now the moft devout devoted
courtier in the long lift of cringing fycophants.
He was the firft in paft times to combat all
ftretches of the prerogative—he is now the
moft furious advocate for its extreme exertion.
He arraigned the ufe of it violently in calling
up to the peerage, a man of a very noble and
illuftrious family †—He now employs it in

* " *What care I for the King's birth-day.*"—Richmond.
† Lord Sackville. He was at the fame time virulently attacked by one of the prefent Secretaries of State, which Secretary, report fays, he is himfelf to fucceed in office, and may
God of his infinite goodnefs make it a true report. There is
an alliance between the virtues. Kick a fpaniel and he fawns
upon you. In return for this contempt the fpirited Sackville
fupports thefe very men *vi et armis*, and his fons in law carried
one of the fulphur and faltpetre addreffes in Ireland, where
fome fad ills befel the family. No man fhould negleft *his own*,
for the fake of a *minifter's bufinefs.*

raifing

raifing upftarts, and borough brokers to the
higher ranks of the nobility. He reveres the
Majefty of the people—and has ftruggled to
reduce them into infignificance, by degrading the only organ through which they can
have any permanent influence. He refpects
the Houfe of Commons---and ftudies to deprive it of its fundamental priviledges.
He has pledged himfelf never to join or
fupport any adminiftration that would not
earneftly endeavour to reform the repre-
fentation---he has never faid one word on
the lofs of Sawbridge's motion, although
the minifter's *dead* majority in the lower
Houfe was two hundred. He is *quite ferious*
for reform---and would employ every man
in England, high and low, poor and rich,
great and little, (women and children *
barely excepted) once every year, upon
the pleafant tafk of parliament choof-
ing. He loves order --- and would place
the link-boy and pick-pocket upon a footing
with the moft refpectable citizen. He values
the dignity and independence of honourable
profeffions---and would fink the great eftablifhment he conducts to the loweft pitch
of fervility. He admires the franknefs of

---

* As an enemy to our fyftem of government I moft earneftly
wifh fuccefs to the *Duke of Richmond's reform*, cordially be-
lieving, that it would of its own natural operation, work the
downfal of this conftitution in a few years ; and perhaps Mr.
Pitt had as well adopt his Grace's plan, as the fcheme in hand,
to effect our *redemption*, as well as to fave his own credit with
the reformers.

a manly

a manly candor---and perfecutes a brave and
venerable officer for giving a free opinion
upon a fyftem of regulations that changed
the whole character of a fphere of fervice
from which the officer derived his reputation
and fortune. ˙ All that remains to complete
his Grace's character, is that he fhould propagate an *Agrarian* principle, and ftrive to˙
equalize the *properties* as well as the franchifes
of men—an atchievement for which the generofity of his own noble nature fits him in
a moft efpecial manner.

IN a word, we have no reafon to dread the
Duke of Richmond?

I AM NOW ARRIVED at the darling
point of my undertaking, to the review of the
youth himfelf, the matchlefs leader of this
mighty hoft! After having engaged fo much
of our attention in the preceding parts of this
pamphlet, you would fuppofe that nothing
more could be faid of Mr. Pitt. Of what
are called his political principles, further
elucidation is without doubt fuperfluous, but
all his perfonalities, thofe appendages of
character which exhibit the mind in the
faithfulleft colours are ftill in a ftate of vir-
ginity, and thefe form a various and fruitful
theme.

EXTRAORDINARY enterprifes can only be
accomplifhed by extraordinary means. The
overthrow of the Britifh conftitution will be
an epoch in the hiftory of this country, and
the

the qualities of the man who effects it, will be an epoch in the hiſtory of the human mind. No man is competent to this grand atchievement who is not capable of inveſting the whole order of moral judgment— who cannot give grace to the groſſeſt deformity, make infection paſs for health, and infanity for wiſdom; confound the intellects of the public, and draw from rank deluſion, the fruits of grave and ſober conviction — in ſhort, who cannot perpetrate with applauſe and triumph what any other man would ſuffer for, upon a ſcaffold or a gibbet.

THE outſet of William Pitt was marked by ſome of the ſtrongeſt features that ever gave an early earneſt of future perfection. In March 1782, he declared himſelf totally unfit for the only civil ſtations he would accept, but by the next July he acquired ſo much knowledge, and the myſteries of government (certainly by inſpiration) became ſo eaſy to him, that he aſcended the moſt laborious office in the Engliſh government without the leaſt ſcruple.

AFTER a long laborious oppoſition, the Whigs were called to the miniſtry, and when they were thought firm in the faſtneſs of power, a cloſet mine was ſprung upon them and down they tumbled. William Pitt after one year's concurrence in their oppoſition, ſteps into their places, chaunts

up

up the old ballad—*Sic vos non vobis*, and tramples them under his feet.

IF after many a bloody ſtruggle in ſome well fought ſiege, an ally ſhould come in the criſis of conqueſt, in the very moment of capitulation, and after a needleſs ſhot or two ſhould take poſſeſſion of the fortreſs—fill his own coffers with the ſpoils of the town, and bind his brows in wreaths of victory, to the utter excluſion of the brave troops and their heroic commander who really fought and conquered—you would call it vile, baſe, and treacherous. It would be ſo in war, and the nation would think it ſo in politicks, had it been the deed of any other man than William Pitt—but in him it was ſpirit and patriotiſm and honeſty! Without affecting a minute analyſis of the moral merit of this act, there was indiſputably that ſtrength of nerve diſplayed in it, that firm contempt of what cold common mortals term fairneſs, that laudable love of power which would demoliſh heaven itſelf to attain its object, that ſtoic reſignation to the imputations of a ſcandalous and ſhabby avarice, that premature apathy to feelings which many a long year of indiſcriminate experience cannot obliterate in vulgar politicians—that this act, (ſingly and independent of any other exploit) confirmed him as one deſtined to ſurpaſs the loftieſt flights of ordinary ambition—as ſomething greater than the greateſt we have yet ſeen!

WHETHER

WHETHER the public, or his immediate connections have carried their predilection for Mr. Pitt to the fartheft extreme, is difficult to determine. The people in fanctioning his proceedings have luckily in fo far altered the fyftem of the Englifh government—his friends in their zeal for him would have changed the whole fyftem of human nature. Their cry has been in the late ftruggle, "charge him with fome crime, " he is pure of all guilt, and therefore the " fitteft man to govern the country."

UNTIL laft year, criminality was thought fo little an adjunct of inexperience, that the counter opinion has ever prevailed. The wickednefs of age, and the innocence of youth, have been allied in moral calculation even to a proverb—" Tell me the oldeft man " in Athens, faid a wife man, and I'll tell " you the greateft rogue."—But proverbs and principles had no weight with the friends of Mr. Pitt.—That the laws of providence were unchangeable—that the principles of creation · were fixed, that human nature was and would ftill be, human nature, were no checks upon their enthufiafm. Even butchers weeped !---Lord Mulgrave himfelf affayed upon his virtues ! --- That Pitt's enemies could not confound the order of God and fubvert the condition of mortality, was in truth fufficient reafon that Pitt fhould be the minifter---for they could not impeach .him.

him although his political life was of *one entire and compleat year's duration*. I say this *has been* the cry, but whether his *second* year does or does not conftitute an exception to thofe theories that fuppofe youth and innocence to be fynonimous, is a knot to be unravelled by others.

FROM the beginning of this reign one great evil has uniformly thwarted the King's friends---the precipitate retreat of the public minifters, when preffed hard by the enemy. Grenville's, Graftons, Shelburne's, feverally furrendered at the call. Even Lord Bute's refiftance was fhort. The indelible crime of Lord North, was his relinquifhing, when the defertion of the Commons was only in profpect.

A PERSON was neceffary as firft minifter, whofe wants made the emoluments of office dear to him—who would ftick to his place like a leech to an impofthume—whofe callous heart could endure the cuffs of the ftruggle, and who had the courageous obtufenefs to treat the cenfure of the Commons like the farcafm of a paragraph. Twice they tried this illuftrious youth, and twice he has afferted an eminence of fuperiority in this moft ufeful of merits. In 1783 he kept the country for fix weeks, and in 1784 for fix months, without any oftenfible government. ---

—*Curruque hæfit refupinus inani,*
Lora tenens tamen.---

He

----He was turned upfide down---trailed along the ground with his head in the mud, but *still kept faft hold of the reins.*

ACUTE infpectors of human life have obferved, that the moft confummate deception is often feen in very young people, and that it arifes not fo much from a contamination of the mind, as an infenfibility to the intrinfic turpitude of that vice from inexperience, and their prodigious facilities in the art of impofition from the confidence generally repofed in them upon a prefumption of their purenefs. I make this remark without any application of it to Mr. Pitt, for he without queftion, comprizes in his own perfon all the virtues of experience and longevity. Not to enter upon any moral difcuffion of it, we know that hippocrify is in truth a minifter's fheet anchor. It is the *fine qua non* of his fituation, and in this admirable quality Lord Shelburne himfelf is the effence of fimplicity compared with Mr. Pitt.

Do you think Lord Shelburne would venture to affure the Commons of England, that his Majefty did *not* mean to diffolve them at the very moment he *did* pofitively mean it? —(The minifter's glory in this refpect muft not be tarnifhed upon an idea that he was only a puppet, and not trufted with the real defign of the cabinet.)

Do you think Lord Shelburne would hazard the farcical negociation of laft February, and

and appear ferious in wifhing a junction with the Whigs at the fame time that his emiffaries were fent to all parts of the kingdom to fecure that very meafure which was intended to prevent a junction? Obferve his lofs and gain by this trick. He only loft thofe untractable animals the country gentlemen—he gained a parliament picked and chofen to his own purpofes, and the celebrity of furpaffing all the minifters that ever went before him in this beft of virtues.

FATE, that favored us in all thefe exigencies, prevented a junction that would certainly have lengthened out the life of this lingering conftitution. The mifcarriage of that treaty is indeed a caufe of triumph—one regret only arifes from its failure. There is a fplendid quality of the human mind which would doubtlefs receive frefh luminations from Mr. Pitt, had he fat in the fame cabinet with Mr. Fox. It is that which Shakefpeare fays turns men's graces into enemies; that fpirit which gangrenes the heart and mortifies the foul at another's merit—which likes a friend while he is contemptible, and hates him in proportion to the growth of his fame and the brilliancy of his exploits—whofe workings are not checked by communion of intereft or unity of fortune, but in the very act of co-operating in the fame caufe and in ftruggling for the fame end, ftudies to degrade

H   its

its fellow labourer.—That fweet refinement of the exterior, that fmooth foft polifh of the mind, which fimpers in your face and choaks with joy at your fuccefs even *then,* when it would undermine your charaƈter, ftop the current of your good fortune, blaft your faireſt laurels, and fink you into barrennefs and beggary.

Poets and politicians excel the reft of the world in this great quality. Its fympathy with the thoufand other virtues which diftinguifh Mr. Pitt, and which feem innate and peculiar to him, affures us that he would throw a number of new graces upon it, had he fat in the fame council with *him,* who of all men living was the moft likely to furnifh him with frequent occafions ; and in this view, moral philofophy may have fuffered by the failure of that junƈtion, but then its tendency to expedite the ultimatum of our wifhes, fuper-atones for every other evil.

The minifter's *manners* in the Lower Houfe form another ground of juft praife.---

We have already fhewn that Mr. Pitt treated the laws and precedents of parliament as the younger Tarquins treated the older— he rode over their body---All the fanƈtities and ceremonies of parliament fhared the fame deferved fate. An affeƈtation there is in vulgar minifters of refpeƈting wherever they find them, certain accomplifhments (as they

are

are deemed) fuch as fcience, learning, wit,
belles lettres, genius.---Even in the moft
determined enemies, thefe endowments have
been reverenced---But this renowned young
man fprings above the level of fuch infirmities, and in his parliamentary manners has
dealt out the moft high and haughty contempt, to fuch members *efpecially* as happened to rank high in public efteem upon
thefe very pretences. You would think on the
firft confideration perhaps, that fuch a man
as Burke was entitled to the ufage of a gentleman. His contributions to the ftock of ufeful philofophy ; his expofition of falfe ethicks,
and falfe polity ; thofe fplendid labours which
augment the literary glory of the nation,
his vaft and varied literature, the number,
the beauty of his compofitions, his age, the
devotion of thirty years to the public fervice, that eloquence which *once* carried his
name covered with admiration to every part
of the empire.---

ADMITTING him to poffefs a hundred times
this merit, it were mere weaknefs to allow
him the leaft quarter : for he is a moft rancorous and remorfelefs enemy to the King's
friends. The illuftrious youth opened the bat-
teries upon him in perfon, and bravely declared
that he defpifed him. * This was the fig-

---

* In debating the King's fpeech when the Marquis of
Lanfdown was Minifter, and Mr. Pitt Chancellor of the Exchequer.

nal

nal for *fyftematic* operation, and fcoffing
Burke with every indignity is now become
a fphere of fervice, a regular channel of promotion. It made *Wrotfley* a general, and
will enoble *Rolle*.

By the fame pitiful calculation you would
prefume, for inftance that, if Sheridan's literary labours were alluded to by this great
minifter, the allufion would be in his praife.
Oh! no—His towering foul is a ftranger to
fuch feelings. For this very excellence in
Sheridan---for an unrivalled fuperiority in one
of the moft difficult exercifes of the human
capacity ;---for that which "young Ammon
" wifhed, but wifhed in vain"—for an
eminence in letters, which made the name
of *Sheridan* refpectable, when the name of *Pitt*
(refplendent as it afterwards became) was
never even heard of—has the noble youth
obliquely taunted him and continued the
practice until a tide of defeats deterred him
from fuch encounters. The minifter is en-
trenched body deep in human nature through
thefe conflicts. The family of Pitt was exalted by perfonal genius, and nothing can be
more reafonable than his jealoufy that any
other man fhould burft from the cloud of
an ill matched fortune, and by dint of parts
erect himfelf into that notice and diftinction,
which the bulk of mankind owe to the labours of feveral men in feveral generations.
" To hate thofe arts that caufed ourfelves to
                          rife,"

rife," is a golden maxim, engraved upon the heart in deep and legible impreffions.

To draw good effects from bad caufes, to derive popularity from real virtue is mere botchery. Give us the man who can extort glory from pofitive wickednefs, and fet the nation blubbering his praifes for an act that deferves their execration. The affair of the *Pells* exhibits a ftriking inftance of this fpecies of merit in this incomparable minifter.

His prefent majefty has the greateft perfonal revenue of any monarch in Chriftendom. Four times however in the courfe of his reign, have the public been obliged to pay his debts : (in the laft payment there has been infinite excellence. His majefty affured the nation when Pitt was minifter before, that he fhould not again prefs upon them in that way ; and preffing upon them in that very way and in lefs than two years, fhews that valiant contempt of folemn declarations which is indifpenfible to a good government.) The magnitude of his income and the extremity of his diftreffes * forced a fufpicion of the integrity of the expenditure, and from a feries of concurring circumftances, this fufpicion grew to fuch a height that granting money to the civil lift and bribing the parliament, were deemed one and the fame thing. The clerkfhip of the **Pells**

* His Lord Steward once told the Houfe of Peers that his majefty had not a loaf of bread for his fupper.

H 3

is

is a very profitable fituation, but never was
confidered as a fit provifion for a chief minifter. No chief minifter ever accepted it, and
William Pitt, on the top of Pifga with the
land of Canaan before his eyes—at the head of
this government and at his time of life, with
all the great finecures of the country in profpect, was not quite fo unhackneyed in the
ways of men as to ftoop to fuch a trifle. No.
He did that which was far more beneficial
in that crifis; he gave the Pells to Colonel
Barre, and threw Barre's penfion of near
four thoufand pounds a year back into the
finking fund of the King's friends—into this
very *civil lift :* and this he did in the heyday
of the parliamentary ftruggle laft winter. I
will admit for a moment with the faction,
that corrupting the Commons is vile and infamous, difgraceful as they fay to the Crown
and the legiflature, but they are blind not to
perceive that the more this is admitted, the
more it enhances the glory of Pitt. Not Fa-
bricius in rejecting the gold of Pyrrhus—nor
Cincinnatus in abandoning empire for poverty,
nor the elder nor the younger Cato were half
fo extolled as William Pitt for this notable
generofity. He was a mirror of difintereft-
ednefs! a model of purity! *Romanis ducibus
et Graiis anteferendus*—fifty cubits beyond any
thing in Greek or Roman ftory !!

FROM the affair of the receipt tax, this
wonderful young man hit off a merit of nearly

ly the same sort. When Lord John intro‑
duced this tax, Pitt praised it extremely;
but when he found it became unpopular, he
judiciously ceased his panegyricks, and Lord
Mahon (his brother in law) laboured daily
in the pace of Jacob, with head and hands
and shoulders, to swell the clamor against it.
Such is the wittol courage of the *faction*, that
in the height of the public phrenzy last win‑
ter, they dared to carry forward a bill to make
this tax effectual and on the 10th of February
upon a discussion of its clauses, the House
demanded Pitt's opinion upon it. The ques‑
tion was put to him in a thousand shapes,
and for several hours before he opened his
lips. It is an admirable part of Mr. Pitt's
parliamentary manners that, though he of‑
ten replies to the question of an individual
member, whenever the body of the House
request an answer from him, he sits as mo‑
tionless and mute as a statue. For a minister
to refuse an answer concerning a public mea‑
sure, is always well---but it is still better that
a finance minister upon a point of finance
should sit speechless. At length however
he declared the tax an admirable one, and
supported it.

THIS contempt of the House was a great
object, but he had a much greater object in
contemplation. The tax in question had
been the chief ground of odium against the
faction. The famous meeting in Westmin‑
ster Hall was advertised for the succeeding

Saturday, and Pitt, with the wifdom of a
profound ftatefman, expected that the electors of Weftminfter would be kindly taken
in by this exquifite cunning, coupled
with a report which had been juft at
that time carefully propagated, that he
meant to repeal it---and that they would of
courfe receive their old favorite Fox with
the more coldnefs. But you would think
perhaps that the perfeverance of the Houfe
defeated Pitt's fcheme—By no means. His
fruitful foul is fraught with expedients. By
the dawn of the day of the Weftminfter
meeting, handbills were difperfed through all
parts of the town, and delivered at the hall
gate to the electors, gravely cautioning them,
" not to credit the mifreprefentations of a
" degraded and defperate faction upon this
" fubject, folemnly affuring the public that
" Mr. Pitt reprobated the receipt tax, and
" that he would moft certainly repeal it."---
What chance have his miferable enemies
againft a minifter fo rich in refources?

PICTURES are often prefented to us by
fanciful writers of a certain noblenefs of
thinking (as it is called) that grows out of
the intrinfic dignity of a great mind---a
grandnefs of thought, which fcorns the
promotion of fame by low artifices, which
defpifes the giddy adulation that impofture
filtches from blinding the multitude, and
the venal flattery which corruption pur-
chafes

chafes from flaves and fycophants, valu-
ing itfelf only upon the fober applaufe re-
fulting from a deliberate canvafs of a man's
real merits ; and thefe pictures I confefs are
very captivating in theory : but conftrained
to fuch a fphere, no minifter would ever
make the impreffion neceffary for *us* in this
great undertaking. The qualifications we
want are the exact reverfe of this picture—
We want a loftinefs that would fnuff the
Heavens at one moment, and a grovelingnefs
that would lick the duft upon the next—
an inflated affumption of purity, thick in
the practice of the rankeft proftitution—a
pompous pretence of neglecting the common
arts of popularity making, when the moft
fhamelefs fhifts, the moft fcandalous devices,
are exerted to extort the perifhable acclaim
of a fingle day.—We want that ufeful pride
which is meannefs in reality—that myfterious
fort of fubtlety which is miftaken for candour
---that pollution which paffes for purity---that
fraud which wears the garb of honefty, and
that fordidnefs and bafenefs which refemble
fpirit and honour. Thefe are the ingredients
to conftitute a true ftatefman. Thefe are the
virtues we want, and in thefe virtues the Al-
mighty has gifted this matchlefs young Minifter beyond the firft of the firft clafs ! !

WHAT does the reader think of old Pitt's
celebrated retort upon Walpole (when Walpole taunted him for his youth) being publifhed during the late ftruggle, in a fhape fo
fingu-

fingularly dextrous as to appear the work of
Pitt the younger---faftening the fuppofition
by annexing a catalogue of brilliant invectives againft the " degraded and the defperate
" faction?" And how publifhed, in pamphlets and news-papers?—No—there the fallacy had been foon detected. Honeft John
Bull was affaulted as he paffed along the
ftreets, with the mantling volume of this auguft Minifter's eloquence ; and gaped with
wonder to fee how Fox was ftruck dumb by
a fpeech, delivered twenty years before Fox
was born !

Not a blank crevice of any dead wall, pe-
deftal, centry-box, or cobler's bulk, in this
great metropolis that was not decorated with
this veritable evidence of the Minifter's capacity. Boluffes, plaifters, pills, draughts,
decoctions, cathartics, clyfters, and cata-
plafms, were all hidden under the vaft
folio of

PITT and the CONSTITUTION.

---Had the Minifter continued the trade a
month longer, the health of the community
had infallibly been refcued from the poifon
of empyrics; the whole tribe of itinerant
doctors muft have'perifhed ; and not a fecond
quack in the country could have procured
a livelihood ! !

PITT (in imitation perhaps of the theologi-
ans, who comprife the effence of moral duties
in four cardinal virtues) concentrates the whole
compafs

compafs of political fcience under four cardinal aphorifms—*viz.* violation of chartered
rights—erecting a fourth eftate in our fyftem
—overturning the well compounded ballance
of this conftitution---and the coalition. Thefe
are his cardinal aphorifms, and whether he
is engaged in defending or attacking, whether he is opening a great meafure of government, or difplaying an adverfary's ignorance,
for faying *or* inftead of *and*, whether puzzled
by his own or his enemy's argument, in
whatever embarraffinents, dilemmas, or
difficulties he finds himfelf, a recurrence to
any of thefe is fure to refcue him. Every
effort of reafon and ridicule has been employed to ficken him from this practice, but
he declares that he *fhall* and that he *will* conti-
nue the cuftom in defpite of both. Thefe
Cardinal aphorifms come home to the bow-
els of the Houfe, and a fonorous bringing
out of either of them, accompanied with
a bounce of the arm and a long look towards the right door of the gallery, is always infallible in procuring a formidable cho-
rus of diffonant but determined *hear hims.*

THEIR political ufes are infinite. After fo
ftoutly refifting the violation of Charters by
other men, who can difpute his right to cut
up the great Charter of the land in the vital
part, or to purloin the Charter of the India
Company in the way that fuits his own purpofes ? Such grace, fuch magic is there about
him,

him, that even in the very act of attacking
Charters, he ftuns the fenfes with the facred-
nefs of Chartered rights---After oppofing
the addition of a new eftate, who can deny
his title to reduce the old eftates? If three
eftates are better than four, by the fame ratio, two are better than three. Expanfion
always relaxes authority, and blending the
powers of the third eftate in the two firft, will
brace the fyftem amazingly---After maintaining "the well compounded balance of the con-
" ftitution," furely the deftruction of the conftitution in toto is his, by right of conqueft.

Towards the accomplifhment of great
events, nothing has a prouder effect than
fanguinary meafures. Blood ftrikes an awe
into men, and fhedding a portion of it gives
a folemn and workmanlike air to a revolution. Even in this fuperior line of merit,
the miniftry have difcovered confiderable capacity, but we are defrauded of their full energy by the littlenefs of the modern character.
Minifters, like men, muft accommodate
themfelves to the genius of their time, and a
legal death in England, may fairly quadrate
with a military maffacre in Rome. The principle that ordered the deftruction of fix legions
in the latter country, was not a fpark more
pure or more noble than the principle which
deftined fix men in the former country to
perifh by the hands of the hangman ; and a
difference in the *fize* of the events is imput-
able,

able, not to the difproportion of faculty in the
ftatefmen, but to the wide difparity of the two
ages. In confining fix men in Newgate, and
then trying them * for a murder, upon the
bribed evidence in all appearance of the real
murderers, there was undoubted and decifive
excellence—but the conduct was moft accomplifhed towards the feventh murderer---the
chief victim of this immolation. He was
fuffered to range the town for fix weeks after
he killed the conftable, as ignorant of the
honour intended him, as the deftined facrifice
in Pope's Effay, and though not literally
" Licking the hand juft raifed to fhed his
" blood,"---was (up to the *very moment* of
being charged in a bill of indictment with
the flaughter of a fellow-creature) fo con-
fident and unwary, that his accufers have all
the glory of that fubtle and finifhed treachery
which fpeaks the utmoft refinement of mind,
undegraded by the fimplicity of fhame, or
the foolifhnefs of remorfe, but altogether
forming that fupreme that fublime villainy
which marks a true genius !

But alas ! the trial was by a jury, and
Buller was not the Judge.

And do you imagine, Mr. Pitt will ever be
detected as authorizing fuch a profecution ?---
He---His high foul fwells with indignation

---

* For the death of Caffon the conftable killed in Covent
Garden.

et the very thought. Do you think *he* ever authorized the High Bailiff of Weftminfter to grant a fcrutiny ? Do you think *he* would tell a peer that the King would deem him an enemy if he voted for the India Bill. Do you think *he* ever bribed any member of the Houfe of Commons ? *(his* undefiled perfon concerned in fuch a bawdy bufinefs!) Oh no.---He has a fecundity of ftratagems upon every exigency, and his own opulent fancy, (without the advantages of his ftation) will never fuffer him to be difconcerted upon fuch occafions.

The beauty of this plot is, that though the profecution was maintained with a moft laudable malignancy, it is univerfally dif-avowed. " When your poffibility has taken " place at the hip, you might as well take " off the head at once, doctor," faid a father once, upon a certain difmemberment which a fon of his had nearly fuffered from a flip of the midwife's forceps.---Had this murderer been hanged, it had been a matter of indiffer-ence to him whether any perfon would avow the thing or not.---Somebody muft have car-ried it on that is certain---and yet, from the firft minifter at Whitehall, to the laft mifcre-ant at the Old Bailey, every fufpectable perfon has pofitively denied any knowledge of it. It was right to deny the profecution fince it failed, but it was the foul of true wifdom to

commence

commence it. Make death the price of friendſhip to a man, and few will perſiſt in ſo hazardous an attachment. All the ſchemes of human life are carried on by confederacy, and if the greateſt are ſtripped of their connections, they become of no avail. When you cannot directly ruin your enemy; the beſt indirect mode is to deſtroy his friends, and had this proſecution ſucceeded, a copious deſertion muſt inſtantly have taken place in the forces of Fox, which conſideration alone is a full juſtification of the attempt. If Fox ſhould (as ſeems likely) ſoon regain his aſcendency over the public; greater than the greateſt of paſt efforts, muſt be tried to lower him. Daggers may be uſed to better purpoſe than threatening the uſe of them in letters :---there are ſurer poiſons than *euphorbium*, and methods of adminiſtering it more infallibly than daſhing it upon a huſtings.

Having ſpoken of Fox, I cannot forbear remarking the fanaticiſm of his friends in daring to lift him into any competition with this wonderful young miniſter, and the better to demonſtrate the madneſs of their zeal, it is worth while to review them both in conꞁtraſt.

THAT TRANSCENDANT CAPAꞁCITY, which qualifies the individual to lead the million, burſt upon the world from both, the firſt moment they ſpoke in the Senate.

But

But their gifts are unequal, and the fuperior endowment of the one is fufficiently attoned to the other, by the moſt fingular ſtrokes of fortune that ever lifted a man prematurely out of his fphere.

AFTER a routine of fervice in moſt of the civil boards of executive government---after fourteen years of long labour, trouble, and toil, Fox attained only a fecondary employment in the King's council.---Pitt got the firſt office in the ſtate after about fourteen months agreeable exercife, without the drudgery of ſtudy, the pain of fubordination, or the fatigue of long endurance.

Fox begun his career under family prejudice, and had a mafs of obſtacles to fubdue. His name likeVefpafian's lineage created hofts of enemies.---

PITT entered upon life in all the eclat of hereditary glory, and had the prepoffeffions of mankind in his favour. The name he bore, like the ſtamp of Pompey's foot, raifed him legions of friends.

Fox is fo bereft of refources, that he has nothing to confide in but his own genius and induſtry. He became a miniſter through the people and their reprefentatives, and has managed fo miferably that he can never hope to regain power by any other courfe. Narrow and circumfcribed in his fphere, he is only a whig—a mere whig.—

PITT confides in a degree to his genius,

and

and induſtry, but he has a ſurer ground of
ſucceſs than both of them. He would have
been a miniſter by the voice of the Commons perhaps by choice, but finding that
road barred up, he took fate as he found
her, and journeyed onward even by the
path-way. He has ſhewn ſuch a dexterity of addreſs, that he may retain or re-
aſcend his preſent dignity, by every method that ever elevated a politician in this
country, without hazard of conſiſtency; and
his creed is ſo comprehenſive that he is
Whig or Tory, both or neither, according
to the preſſure of neceſſity.

Fox is encumbered with paſſion without
acerbity, and diſcovers all the infirmities of
human nature in the courſe of a diſcuſſion.
Guided by the impulſe of his heart, his
temper varies with the variation of his ſubject, without guard or diſcretion. He ſome-
times yields up a point with an indecent
facility, but ſtruggles for a principle with
as uncouth and violent a zeal as if he ſtrug-
gled for his exiſtence.—

PITT is graced by acerbity without any
paſſion, and manifeſts the moſt philoſophic
equanimity in the moſt intereſting debate.
Undiſtorted by the barbariſm of feeling, his
mind maintains an even tenor of uniformity,
and he paints the miſeries of an empire, and
the miſplacing of a comma, preciſely under

I   the

the fame animation. He never gives up a point without fome conflict, but then he furrenders principles with a moft placid and gentleman-like complaifance.

Fox rafhly affaults the enemy in his ftrongeft entrenchment, and is never contented with lefs than the cruel delight of feeing his antagonift lay dead at his feet.——

PITT feeks the fafer glory of cutting off a ftray detachment, and never rifks an encounter in the front: like a judicious Polemic he combats the flips and digreffions of an argument, and has the charitable felf-denial to be perfectly fatisfied if he fcratches the furface without in the leaft molefting the vital parts.

Fox has the rudenefs to difdain the ufe of ornament in his fpeeches. He employs words only to convey his meanings, and is always impatient to get rid of them. The ftudy of his foul is to demonftrate his pofitions, and he has fuch an unpolifhed averfion to redundancy, that in his zeal to avoid it, he checks himfelf in the ufe of graces that flow in fpontaneoufly upon his elocution.---

PITT with more fkill carefully confults the great object of found. His words are the moft fhewy which the language affords him, and he dwells upon each, like Narciffus upon his own image. His fpeeches, like the portrait of a young painter, are always high

high-coloured, and if he does not convince you with the folid force of his reafoning, he at leaft compofes you with the flumbering fuavity of his phrafes.

THE infecundity of the former, compared to the latter is moft glaring. Fox has not the faculty to fay three words upon a fubject which he does not underftand. He never afpires above plain fimple terms, and is fo vulgar as to be comprehenfible to the meaneft capacity. He puts his argument indeed into a variety of lights, but then his fterility is fuch, that he feldom adds a word more than is fufficient to exprefs his fenfe.---

PITT on the contrary is inexhauftible and endlefs. He will at any given time, upon any given fubject, make a moft fplendid fpeech, embellifhed with gaudy fhining fentences admirably concatenated, and a feries of fucceffive parenthefes, knit together with a moft fcholaftic punctuation—entirely difburthened at the fame time of the fmalleft * knowledge of the point in difpute. He is often fo lofty and fublime that feveral of the moft acute of his hearers, nay fome of his own country gentlemen have very frankly confeffed, that he actually went above their underftanding. He has the happieft talent

---

* He made three very fine fpeeches againft an objection of Sheridan's upon the Game Act, and at the end of the third, afked Sheridan what his objection was,

at amplitude, and will with incredible eafe to himfelf, employ fix times the number of words of any other man, in conveying the fame meaning.

PITT excels in the rancorous feverity of his invectives and the fplendor of his diction :---

Fox only in the fulminations of oratory and an invincible ftrength of reafoning.

To be blind to ones own merit is to be fupremely foolifh, and nothing furely is more exorbitant than to hope others will rate us highly if we do not rate ourfelves fo. Fox fins againft the grain of this good maxim. Whilft others think his genius places him at the head of mankind, his own demeanor is fo miferably unaffuming that he would pafs upon a ftranger for a perfon of little note.

PITT never trufts the delicate tafk of afferting his own worth, even to his beft friends : and every word, deed, and declaration judicioufly convey, that he thinks himfelf (what he moft certainly is)—the greateft man in all the world !!

IF power be precious, to furrender it haftily is the worft rafhnefs, and no man is worthy of it who does not prove its value by a luft of procuring and a reluctance at parting it. Fox was always difplaced by intrigues ; but he retires from office with as unfeeling an indifference, as if it was not

worth

worth keeping.---No intrigue and no treachery could affect the mind of Pitt. He bravely refifted a battery of fix weeks cenfures from the Commons of England, and never gave up his ftation until he was kicked off the Treafury bench.

In every perfonal view the fuperiority of Pitt is unqueftionable. A confcience that can digeft a direct breach of the moft folemn engagement, and a total obliteration of every fenfe of gratitude when occafion requires, are the moft ufeful attributes of a ftatefman. In thefe qualities Fox is glaringly defective. He has never been honoured with a reproach for *private* perfidy, his mind cannot afpire to the dignity of a breach of *public* faith, and the meaneft perfon that contributed to his exaltation has never accufed him with an oblivion of favor.---

Pitt fcorns the diminutive graces of perfonal treachery, his huge foul pants for larger glory. A fignal deception of the moft auguft affembly in England is alone worthy his capacity, and his vaft ambition is clogged by no embarraffments from gratitude to thofe who promoted him. The firft act of his Miniftry (except betraying the Commons) was to difgrace the very perfon* whofe hardyhood caufed his own elevation, and he is faid to have lately given a fpeci-

---

* The Marquis of Buckingham.

I 3

mea

men of this virtue to the firft perfon in the nation---nay to thofe " who are greater than " the throne itfelf!" Fifteen years before his time he was called to one of the firft offices in the Britifh government by the Earl of Shelburne, and in return, he has laid this nobleman upon the fhelf, to grow reverend from ruft, like a piece of virtu.

Fox without power or fortune has a vaft body of adherents, and fo inveterate is their attachment, that oppreffion and treachery againft their leader only ferve to encreafe their fidelity---

PITT has a furer pledge of loyalty, he has place and patronage, and while he continues Minifter will always command a hoft of followers.

THE external manners of Fox are the moft unguarded imaginable. What ftains not the private man, in his judgment, deforms not the public man. He facrifices to the fex with as little difguife as if the thing were not unfafhionable, and would take a favourite Gabriel by the arm, with as carelefs a fincerity as the fourth Henry of France, or the fifth of England.---

MALIGNITY itfelf can impute no fuch fcandal to Mr. Pitt.

A FROWARD declaration of principles is very indifcreet in a Minifter, for the time may come when it may be expedient to re-
nounce

nounce all principles whatever. Fox carries
this weaknefs to the moſt ridiculous extreme.
He boaſted himſelf the Miniſter of the people, he juſtified the refumption of violated
truſt from Kings, and had the audacity to
vindicate the Revolution, when ſeated upon
the Treaſury bench.---

PITT with more judgment, boaſted himſelf " the miniſter of the crown." Of
Kings and revolutions his prudence kept him
filent, but then he arraigned the refumption
of violated truſt from a company of trading
monopoliſts, with a moſt determined ſincerity.

THEIR India bills reflect an infinity of lights
upon theſe two ſtateſmen. Fox broke the
charter of the company openly without their
conſent. — Pitt broke it cunningly with
their conſent. The former placed the authority at home, where its defects might
be remedied upon diſcovery, which would
be very fatiguing. --- The latter lodged it in India, the ſcene of every iniquity,
where the evil is compleated, before we have
the pain of hearing one word about it. Fox
ſhewed no invention in his ſyſtem. He
only went upon the common acknowledged
principles of government and placed the execution in the few, the controul in the many.
---Pitt's ſyſtem diſcloſed a mine of invention. He proceeded upon a plan, truly original, and dextrouſly inverted all the received
principles of political ſcience. He gave the

I 4   execu-

execution to the many, and the controul to the few. Fox placed the patronage not in the Crown whose influence was already too exorbitant, *by the word of parliament*---not in the Company who had already abused it, *by the word of parliament*; but in a body of men whose unfortunate honesty was their only hope of safety---for this disposal of it roused the vigilance of the whole nation (a temper always injurious to government) and their ruin was infallible upon perverting this influence, opposed as they would be to a certainty, by the Crown, the Peers, and the Company, and perhaps by the public — accountable! responsible! punishable !—

PITT placed the patronage in those very bodies where parliament forbad it, and with great skill rendered it their mutual interest to connive at their mutual abuse of it ; securing the indemnity of both under the obscureness of their operations, and the difficulty of being detected. The dispensers of the India Patronage under this bill, backed by the Crown, the Peers, the Commons, and the Company, may defie the malice and enmity of the whole kingdom.

Fox's bill was conceived in the very selfishness of intellectual pride. It was constituted so arrogantly perfect in its component parts, that no room was left for the skill of parliament. Its efficacy to the government

of

of India was never once difputed, and it
paffed the Commons without one material
change.---

Pitt's bill, on the contrary, was founded with a view to the flattery of parliament.
It was entirely calculated to try their fkill
at polifh and amendment, and (excepting the
trial by Jury, and the difpofal of the patronage) paffed into a law, as radically tranf-
muted as Sir John Cutler's worfted ftock-
ings. Its experience fince it paffed, gives
us the delicious hope of having the amufe-
ment of new alterations in it, every new feffions, which will happily furnifh debates for
the regifters! paragraphs for the prefs! converfation for the public! and comments for
all Europe !!

Fox impudently reprobated the India
delinquents. He defied their power, and fell
a victim to it.—

Pitt reprobated them alfo with a moft
plaufible gravity, but then he fecured their
fupport by a moft fingular addrefs; and
though perhaps he refufed a title to Haftings
(for Haftings has ferved him) he crouches
to his creatures, with the moft engaging con-
defcenfion.

Success is the teft of all human excellence, and by this infallible criterion, my
hero furpaffes his rival beyond the prefumption of parallel---*Fox's bill was the inftrument*

of

*of his down-fall---Pitt's bill confirmed his exal-
tation.*

THE fame fate characterizes the coalitions
that each of them has formed. Fox begun
his political life under Lord North. He
ferved with him in the Admiralty, Treafury,
Pells, &c. After a formidable oppofition
of eight years, and when America (Heaven
blefs the King and his friends) had ceafed to
be any object here, he joined Lord North
(whofe alliance was courted at the fame
time by that cabinet of which Pitt was a
chief member)---exactly as Cicero joined
Antony, and Chatham Newcaftle. — This
coalition is juftly deemed bafe, vile, and infamous.---

PITT joined men whom he oppofed during the *whole* of his political life, and very
charitably allied himfelf to that clofet cabal,
againft whom he imbibed an hereditary
hatred.---That very cabal whofe uniform
aim was the deftruction of his father---who
difgraced him in the year fixty-one, deceiv-
ed him in fixty-five, dishonoured him into
a title in fixty-fix, and after plucking off the
plumage of his popularity, abandoned him
foon after to the fhame they betrayed him
into, and left him to pine the remainder of
his days in penance and mortification.—
This coalition is very juftly deemed wife,
and virtuous, and holy !!

HAVING given this contraft of thefe rival
politicians (a contraft too long, I fear, for
the

the reader, though too fhort for the occafion) what is it, I may afk, but the moft frantic folly that can infect the advocates for Fox, with any idea of his equal competency with Pitt to the government of [this empire, when (independant of Pitt's amiable defigns upon the conftitution, and without bringing any one *good* quality to his aid) his very vices are abfolutely more beneficial to him, than his beft virtues to Fox ?

The fame fuperiority diftinguifhes the literary advocates of the miniftry. The writers for the faction are fhallow fellows, who cannot go beyond a paltry fcrap of wit, or a barren fact. A direct attack they feldom venture, but fkulk into obliquity, and hide in implication. The miferable advantage their poor productions would yield them, had they been written in an upright ftraight forward ftile, is utterly loft: for a jack pudding reader muft think they are abfolutely labouring for their enemies. But the minifterial writers difdain to cripple their cenfures or invelope their meanings. There is a probity in their ftile which will not defcend to the fraud of impofing on their reader. In them you find bone, and nerve, and mufcle, and marrow. They give the faction to the world in its true colours. " Rogues, rafcals, renega-
" does, robbers, raggamuffins, fcoundrels,
" fwindlers, fharpers, brutes, beafts, bank-
" rupts,

" rupts, blackguards, thieves, liars, knaves,
" gamblers, villains, and vagabonds." Here
are titles that terrify, *verba spumantia*, names
that strain the buccinatory muscles, and stag-
ger the very utterance.---Perhaps you would
think it as well to say nothing of their *ingenuity*, but there I beg pardon. A writer
of the most singular ingenuity has lately
entered the lists for the administration.

I WILL give the reader the full scope of
his fancy—let him take in the whole circle
of crimination, let him peruse all the re-
gisters of sin, from the Bible to Hill's Ser-
mons, and all the anathemas thundered out
from Ernulphus down to my Lord Chancellor;---and in all these researches, he will, I
maintain it, find nothing half so curious or
half so apposite, as the crime which this
writer brings home to the coalition ministry.
It is neither more nor less than a positive
charge of SECRET INFLUENCE — of
Secret Influence without conceit or qualifi-
cation. By the most miraculous penetra-
tion, he has discovered an exact parallel between the bigotted favouritism of Edward,
and of Richard the Second, to Despencer
and the Duke of Ireland, and his present
Majesty's dear and loving attachment to the
coalition ministers : namely, to the *Duke of
Portland,* to *Lord North,* and to *Charles Fox.*
It matters not whether these princes admir-
ed or abhorred their servants—whether they
gene-

generoufly adhered to them with the good faith of gentlemen, and the honour of Kings, or bafely betrayed them with the treachery of ruffians—this infpired writer has made the thing as plain as St. Paul's Cathedral.

THE other parts of his performance are exactly of a piece with the above. *My* zeal for the King's friends has impelled *me* to great lengths; yet the rankeft Toryifm recommended or recorded in my pamphlet, is high treafon compared with the tenets of this invaluable politician. He tells us what is certainly true, that our only hope centers in the executive power—that it is fhameful the King cannot command money otherwife than by begging it from Parliament.—That the Civil Lift Reform bill was an impudent infringement upon the influence of the crown.—That the debts contracted by eftablifhing the revolution, and by reducing the power of Lewis XIV. were not worth the acquifition—that the victories under the Duke of Marlborough and Lord Chatham were ferious injuries— that the electors of the kingdom are a fet of corrupt mifcreants—that the late Houfe of Commons was a herd of knaves—and that all the virtue and wifdom of the Englifh nation, is depofited in the Houfe of Lords.

LOOK afkance at the beft man living, and he will feem deformed, fay the philofophers, —furvey the worft with complacency, and you will find graces about him. This liberal line

has

has been adopted by this excellent writer. He has cited the moſt furious meaſures of the Houſe of Commons, in the moſt furious of times, contraſted with the amiable ſtruggles of the hereditary repreſentatives of the peo- ple; he demonſtrates the vice of the demo- cratic branch, points out the expediency of its demolition, and proves beyond all doubt, that the Lords alone deſerve our confidence.

ALL the importance that a ſyſtem of rea- ſoning can derive from the dignity of the reaſoner is due to this pamphlet. Had the reviler of the Houſe of Commons been ſome reprobate vomited forth by that Houſe as unfit to ſit in it.—Had the reviler of the electors been a wretch of *ſuch* a complexion, that the moſt profligate ſet of vote-mongers in the corrupteſt borough throughout the country would not touch with a tongs—the force of his calumnies might have been ſome- what impaired. But when the reader knows his name, and knows that it is a man of that *Romaniſm* of ſoul, which would not con- taminate itſelf by entering ſuch a ſink of filth as the Houſe of Commons—a man of the moſt ſplendid reputation, and the moſt un- ſullied honour—who has no aſperities from diſappointment, no mortifications from the world's contempt—but who in the pleni- tude of conviction, in the fulneſs of ſym- pathy, engages cordially in this great cauſe—when the reader learns that the
author

author of this pamphlet · is · *Sir William Meredith* himself; its doctrines, precious before, will acquire a tenfold value upon that rapturous information!

SIR William Meredith is the man who has thus figured under the ministerial standard—fit client for such patrons!—Unfortunate Burke*, thy laurels now indeed are blighted! *infelix atque impar congreſſus Achilli* —oppoſed by ſuch a combatant as Sir William Meredith, thy fall is certain!

THIS tranſcendent merit ſurely can never paſs unrewarded under ſuch a miniſtry. Sir William has ſervices to recount, and merits to plead, beſide his political abilities. A peerage is the leaſt he deſerves for his invectives againſt the Commons, and he is qualified for that dignity by all thoſe graces that characteriſe ſome wealthier candidates for the ſame honour! Defects of fortune may be ſupplied from the privy purſe, and Sir William can then puſh forward the cauſe in the full force of all his powers, for he is bleſſed with a variety of faculties, and is not confined to common channels in exhibiting his genius: *idoneus arti cuilibet.*

ONE omiſſion only is obſervable in Sir William Meredith's pamphlet. The defamation of the heir apparent ſeems the chief aim of the miniſterial writers, and Sir William has groſly neglected it. His next

---

* SIR William attacks a pamphlet of Mr. Burke's with infinite genius and ſkill.

aſſay will, however, I doubt not, make
amends for that unpardonable informality.

THIS PRINCE's NAME ſuggeſts to me
the deſperateneſs of our condition, ſhould this
conſtitution ſurvive the preſent reign. Alas!
what chance of happineſs could we have under
ſuch a King as the preſent heir of the Engliſh
crown. A Prince conſtituted as his aſſociates
ſay, of every thing inauſpicious to our beſt
wiſhes, without deceit, duplicity, or any of
the other kingly virtues requiſite to the
furtherance of this great ſcheme — who
feels the zeal of a rank Whig for this
conſtitution—whom Whig topics and Whig
characters conſtantly engroſs—who is weak
enough to venerate the principles that raiſed
his family to the Britiſh throne, and to
love their deſcendants, who accompliſhed
that daring change — who neither cants
nor affects to cant.— whoſe faults like his
virtues are the faults of a man — open in-
genuous, undiſguiſed—whoſe character is
pictured in his face, whoſe heart ſpeaks in
his words—who regards a friend with the
ſincerity of an equal, and is as cautious of
his good faith, as if he were not deſtined
for a diadem—who ſoftens the prince with
the urbanity of the gentleman, and exalts the
gentleman with the graces of the prince!

THIS is their repreſentation who know
him beſt, and curſed with our preſent
plagues,

plagues, our miferies would fure be endlefs under *his* fucceffion. Surrounded by a hoft of Whigs, and contaminating the land with Whig principles, not one hope would remain for *us*.

Heu ftirpem invifam et fatis cóntraria noftris Fata Phrygum.—— —

DILLIGENCE and activity in our feveral fpheres may now fave us and our pofterity from this calamitous entail. Seafon and opportunity favour us. The people (pretend the faction what they may) the people I affirm, are decidedly with us. That the Pitt epidemic is cured, is now the enemy's cry,---but the Pitt epidemic is *not* cured. Miferable philofophers are they indeed who think the public mind flies from reafon, and recurs to it again, with the fame celerity. In decency to themfelves, the people cannot difgrace the part they have fo lately acted, by fo early a recantation, nor defert the dear youth until (by his ftriking a great blow in the lucky crifis) their defertion only provokes his ridicule. The nation, in truth, appears fick of this conftitution. The love of liberty is openly ftigmatized as a hair-brained whimfical reverie. A deluge feems to have over-run the country, and happily fwept away fenfation, intelligence, and fpirit. Public ignorance is ever favourable to the defigns of power.

   " Fools grant whate'er ambition craves,
   " And men, once ignorant, are flaves."

K   *That*

That indeed is the golden hour of opportunity, and this paroxifm we have luckily attained. Defpotic monarchs, and enflaved countries are the themes of our admiration —free ftates and freedom the but of our ridicule. That brilliant flame of national contempt for America, which for ten years before the American war pervaded this nation,* which fubjected every man who ventured a word in vindication of the colonies, to a fufpicion of treafon againftthe prefent ftate, and which fortunately fevered us from fuch defpicable wretches—flourifhes at this moment as vigoroufly as ever againft that country. A portion of the fame laudable fentiment prevails towards Ireland, as blindly ignorant at the fame time of the real difeafe of Ireland, as if Ireland lay under the North Pole. As to the Dutch, the nation is bravely burfting with hatred againft them, and why? —Becaufe we were never at war with them before the year eighty-one—becaufe Empires are cemented by the faith that binds individuals—

---

* Profeffed hoftility to America had the fame fuccefs in the general elections of 1768 and 1774, with profeffed *Pittifm* in the late elections; which fact by the way, imparts an additional grace to the illuftrious youth's invectives againft Lord North for the American war.

—— " The people's voice is old; It *is*, and it is *not*, the voice of God."

becaufe the Dutch fhould not in decency
eat, drink, fleep, grow fat, take phyfic ****
or **** without our fpecial leave : *for that*
we helped them into independence two hundred years ago—from our enmity to Philip
II. and affifted them in retaining that inde-
pendance one hundred years ago—from the
neceffity we felt of humbling Lewis XIV.
And as if the Dutch common-wealth was
of no more weight in the fcale of Europe
than the Englifh Commons in the fcale of
the Englifh conftitution, this nation burns
againft that people, with the rational revenge
of a fchool-boy fcratched by his play-fel-
low.

An obvious good fortune may refult to
the miniftry from the embarraffments of
Holland. In reward of the treacherous
friendfhip of France, it is poffible the Dutch
may yield up fome of their Eaftern territories, and the French, aided by the Indian
princes, (who *all* hate us mortally) may
perhaps exterminate the Englifh completely
from Afia. The miniftry (their cares being
then condenfed to the management of this
ifland fingly) will not be diverted by external
objects ; and we may indeed hope to have
our happinefs eftablifhed upon a folid bafis.

This is indeed a confummation devoutly
to be wifhed ; and in the contemplation of it
I fhall now take my leave of the reader : in-
voking the genius of monarchy, that is,
the

the spirit of good government, to illumine his understanding, as it has enlightened mine—that he may be induced to give his portion of aid to further the general felicity of human nature, and the particular happiness of his native country---by supporting this Ministry with might and main !!

For myself, I have only one thing to exact from the reader---that wherever I have failed to do full justice to the present Administration, he will impute the defect to lack of parts, and not of zeal for their success--- And if hereafter, when this crooked fabric shall be erased to the ground, the meanest man should attribute to my panegyricks any promotion of that great event, in *such* a cause the slightest praise will outweigh an immortality in any other, and I shall with truth exclaim in the words of the poet :

Sublimi feriam sidera vertice.

London, *January* 22, 1785.

F I N I S.